The Australian

Roof Building
Manual

Pinedale Press

Published by Pinedale Press
Illustrations and text by Lloyd Hiddle & Allan Staines

National Library of Australia
Cataloguing-in-publication data
© Lloyd Hiddle
© Allan Staines

The Australian Roof Building Manual
National Library of Australia card no. and ISBN 0 9593024 9 2

 All rights reserved. No part of this book may be
reproduced, stored in a retrieval system or transmitted in
any form or by any means, electronic, electrostatic,
mechanical, photocopying, recording or otherwise without
permission in writing from the Publishers.

Publisher and Copyright Holders:
Pinedale Press
2 Lethbridge Ct., Caloundra 4551 Qld. Australia.

1st Edition	July	1988
Reprint	Nov.	1988
Reprint	Jan.	1990

Disclaimer

*Since all information is a general guide only and has
been given in good faith and in no way replaces
Commonwealth or Local Building requirements and
the need for individually prepared plans and
specifications, no legal responsibility will be
accepted by the Authors or Publisher (including
liability for negligence) should the information or
advice be incorrect, incomplete, inappropriate, or in
any other way defective.*

Contents

Author's Notes

A great satisfaction and highlight for an apprentice is finally being able to successfully cut out and pitch a roof.

It is the intention of the authors to help the apprentice in reaching this goal and to speed up the task for the tradesman carpenter by providing quick and easy tables and ready to set bevels. Whilst Sections 3 and 5 on marking and erecting rafters give some description on obtaining lengths and shortening of particular rafters, obtaining lengths and shortening of all rafters has been included in section 7 for quick and easy reference.

The contents of this manual are regularly updated and submissions are invited where simpler or better methods can be substituted.

Please write to the Publisher.

Allan Staines

Alfred C. Dickel

Simple Roofing Basics

Roof Designs

Today's architecture ranges from traditional and colonial to ultra modern and contemporary design.

The roof of a building is seen by Designers as one of the most important features, for the slope and shape of a roof can change the whole appearance of the building. It is, therefore, the part of a building which is most subject to the Designer's creativity.

Some common variations are shown incorporating the 'run' and 'rise' of the slope together with advantages and disadvantages of each type.

Skillion & lean-to roofs are simpler to construct but increase the cost of the overall construction time and materials because walls must be built to varying heights. To reduce roof framing costs, rafters may be applied as purlins running across the roof rather than down the slope as a rafter would normally. This eliminates the need for battens. Their spacings may be increased by using thicker roof cladding.

Skillion & (Lean-to Roof)

Gable roofs are always attractive and are a simple roof to pitch requiring neither hips nor valleys. However, one disadvantage is that the gable ends (or gable end walls) increase house maintenance unless of brick or a non paint surface.

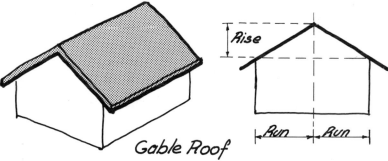

Gable Roof

Dual pitched roofs are usually applied to split level houses. The roof is basically two separately pitched skillion roofs usually with a variation in both the rise and the run.

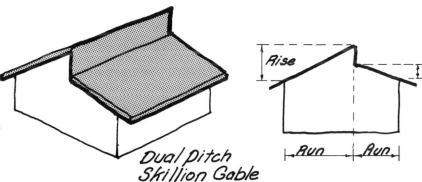

Dual Pitch Skillion Gable

Cont

Unequal pitch gable roofs are a modern variation of the traditional gable.

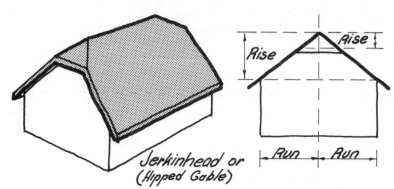

Unequal Pitch Gable Roof

Jerkinhead or hipped gables are often used to visually reduce an overly high gable end.

Jerkinhead or (Hipped Gable)

The Dutch Gable is a combination of the hip and gable. Care should be taken to adequately waterproof the points where the hips meet the gable and where the roof line meets the vertical face of the gable.

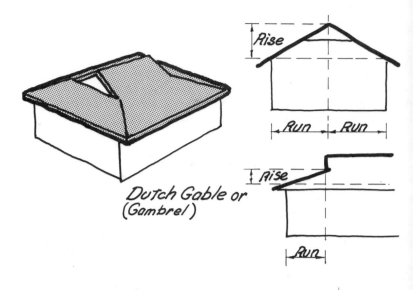

Dutch Gable or (Gambrel)

The Hip or Hip and Valley roof reduces overall house maintenance.

Hipped Roof

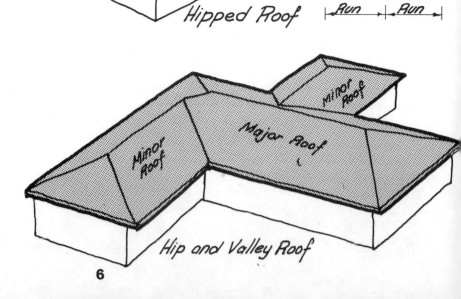

Hip and Valley Roof

Roofing Members & Where They Fit

Hip Rafter
A rafter used to form the intersection between two sloping surfaces of a roof meeting at an external corner.

Common Rafter
The main sloping rafter in a roof spanning between wall plates and ridge.

Ridge
The horizontal member against which the top ends of rafters are fixed.

Broken Hip
A main hip rafter which is shortened by the interference of a minor offset roof. It spans between the end of a main ridge and minor ridge/valley intersection.

Cripple Jacks
Rafters which are cut to fit between a valley rafter at their lower ends and a hip or broken hip at their top ends.

FIG 1

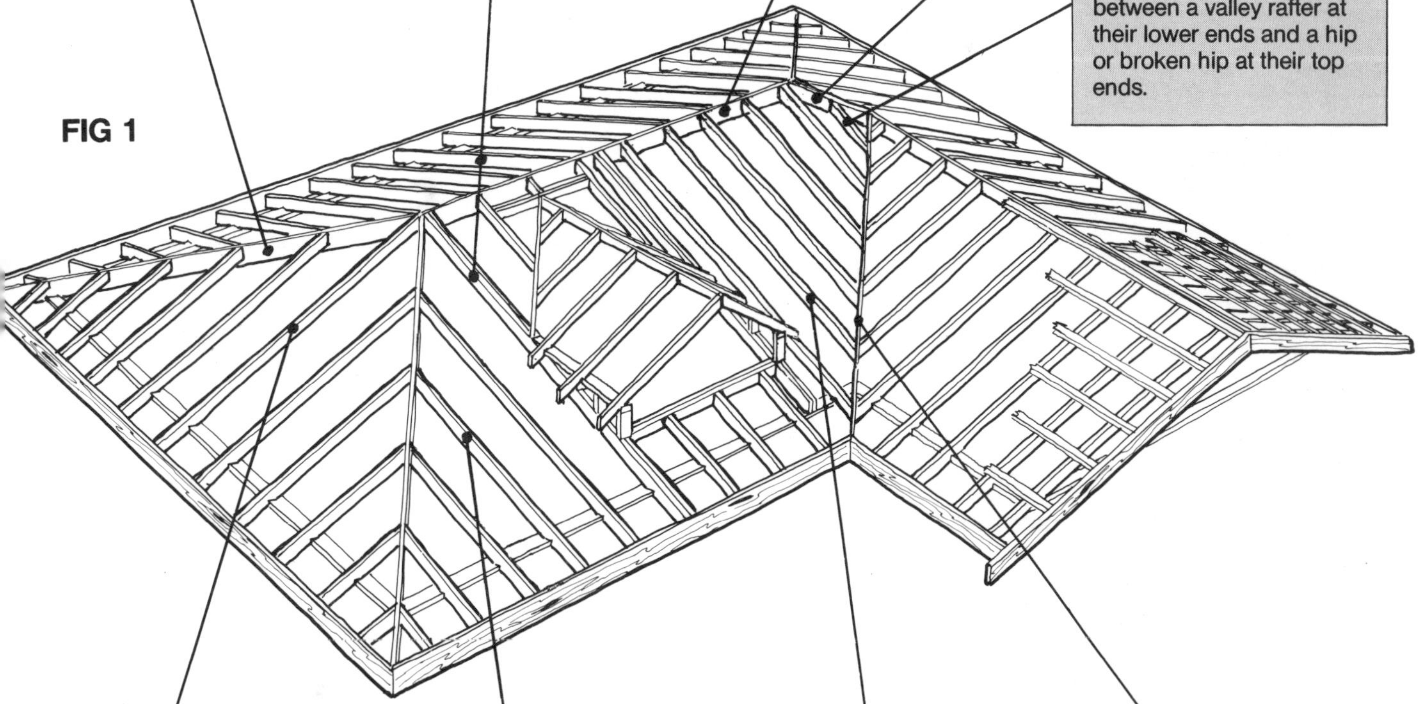

End Jack
A common rafter pitched from the centre of the end wall plate span to the intersection of the hips and ridge.

Hip Jacks
Rafters spanning between the top wall plate and hip. They are installed in pairs against each side of the hip.

Valley Jacks
Rafters which are cut to fit against a valley rafter at their lower end and against a ridge at their top ends.

Valley Rafter
A rafter used to form the intersection between two sloping surfaces of a roof meeting at an internal corner.

Roofing Terms (See Figs 2 & 3)

Span
The overall horizontal distance across the roof measured from the outside edges of the top wall plates. See fig 2.

Run
When a roof has the same slope on each side, the run will be half the span. See fig 2.

Rise
The vertical measurement of an inclined member. The rise of a roof is measured vertically from the top of the wall plate to the point where the backing lines intersect. See fig 2.

Backing Line
A line taken from the outside edge of top wall plate and extended to the centre of the roof at the slope angle of the roof. The length of the backing line represents the geometrical length or length of rafter given in the tables. See fig 2.

Slope or Pitch
The angle of inclination that the roof makes with a horizontal line. See fig 2. The angle of the slope is dealt with on page 10.

Bevel
An angle applied to a roof member for the purpose of cutting and fitting against other members.

Birdsmouth
The removal of a triangular piece from the underside of a rafter to provide a horizontal seat for the rafter to rest on the top wall plate. This is called a birdsmouth. See fig 3. The position of the backing line of a rafter determines the depth of the birdsmouth. See page 15.

The Triangle Makes it Easy

All sloping roofs are based on a right angle triangle shape. Each rafter in a roof can boast of its own right angled triangle with the horizontal base representing the *run* of the rafter: the perpendicular height representing the *rise* of the rafter: and the hypotenuse or sloping side of the triangle representing the *length* of the rafter. See fig 2. In a typical roof of equal pitch, the triangle representing the common rafter will have its base as half the span of the building (called the *run)*; its perpendicular height as the height of the roof above the top wall plate (called the *rise)* and its hypotenuse as the sloping plane or the rafter itself. Fig 4A shows a common rafter triangle.

The Run

If each rafter is imagined to be part of a triangle, then the run of the rafter can easily be identified. It is the run which is the important factor when calculating lengths. For calculating purposes, the sectional size of rafters may be disregarded. Fig 4B shows the plan view of the hip roof taken from fig 4A and indicates the run of each triangle.

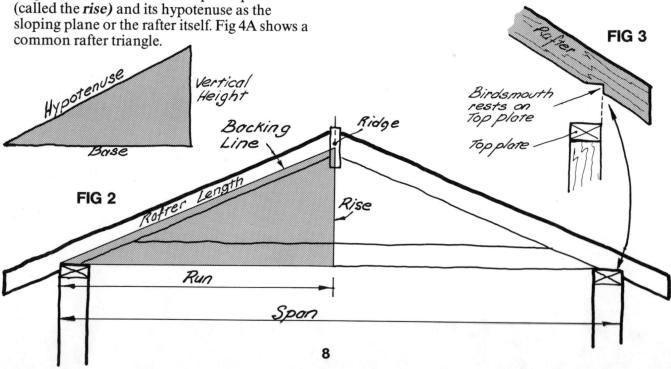

FIG 2

FIG 3

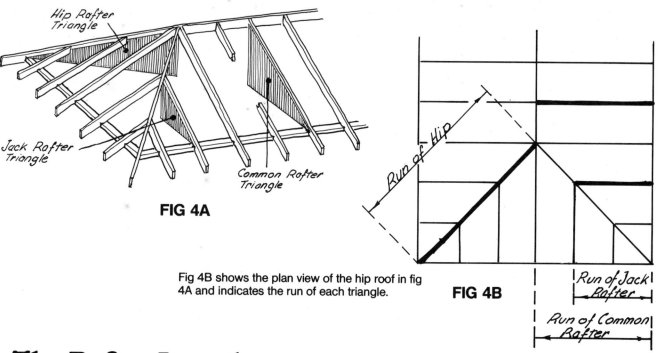

Fig 4B shows the plan view of the hip roof in fig 4A and indicates the run of each triangle.

FIG 4B

The Rafter Length

As explained, the hypotenuse of the triangle represents the length of the sloping rafter. This sloping line can be defined as the 'geometrical length' of the rafter. The length is obtained from the tables and marked on the rafter. This length is then shortened to allow for the thickness of the members to which the rafter is going to be attached. This shortened length is known as the 'cutting length'.

For Example:

The common rafter is attached to the ridge. The geometrical length of the common rafter arrives at the centre of the ridge. See figs 2 & 5. Therefore the tables lengths will have to be reduced by half the thickness of the ridge. Likewise, all rafters have to be reduced to allow for the thickness of the members to which they are attached. For marking out rafters, refer to section 3.

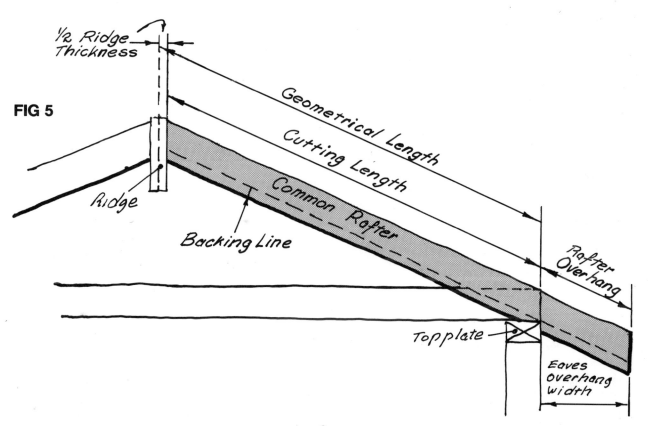

FIG 5

9

The Slope

Working drawings or specifications will provide information on the slope or pitch of the roof. This may be stated in one of the following forms:

1. Angle in degrees. See fig 6.
2. Ratio of the rise to the run. See figs 7A & B.
3. Rise per unit run. See figs 8 A & B.

The angle in degrees method is used throughout this book as it is the most commonly used and the most easily understood and recognized. However, the other 2 methods are included in the tables should they be required. See below for a clearer explanation of each method.

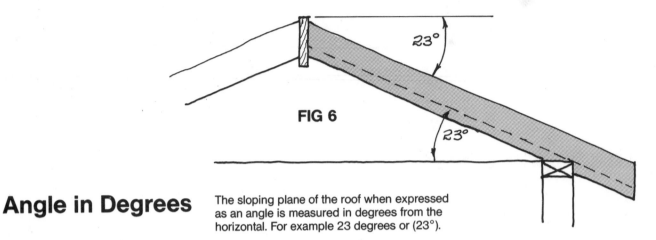

FIG 6

Angle in Degrees

The sloping plane of the roof when expressed as an angle is measured in degrees from the horizontal. For example 23 degrees or (23°).

FIG 7A

FIG 7B

Ratio of the Rise to the Run

A ratio of 1:3 indicates a rise of 1 metre for every 3 metres of run, or a ratio of 3:1 indicates a rise of 3 metres for every 1 metre of run.

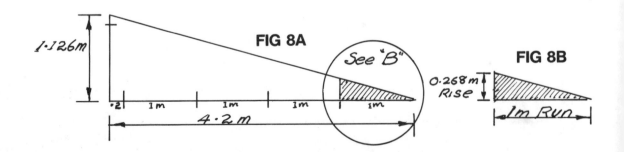

FIG 8A

FIG 8B

Rise Per Unit Run

A rise per unit run of 268 describes a roof slope of having a vertical rise of 268mm for every metre of run. A run of 4.2m will have a vertical rise of 1.126m (4.2m x 268mm = 1.126mm).

Marking Out the Top Plates & Ridge

For Hip Roofs

Top Plates

Step 1   Determine the roof span and measure out from the corners marked "A" the distance A-X. This represents half span. Mark these positions on the top plates.

Step 2   Mark out the thickness of the first common rafter and end jack rafters. These are located centrally over the half span "X" lines. See fig 9.

Step 3   From these positions commence setting out rafter spacings towards the building corners. Do not be concerned if the end spacing is shorter. It is good practice to allow an extra jack rafter approximately 150mm-200mm from the corner for added strength and support.

Step 4   Common rafter positions along the ridge board can be equally spaced but do not exceed the maximum spacing specified in the plans.

Ridge   To mark rafter positions on the ridge, lay the ridge across the ceiling joists or top plates and transfer the applicable rafter positions directly across. Square these marks onto both sides of the ridge. See fig 12A.

Ridge Lengths   For how to obtain ridge lengths see pages 11 & 38.

Hip Roof

FIG 9   Set out first common rafters and end jack rafters first. These are all measured half span from the corners.

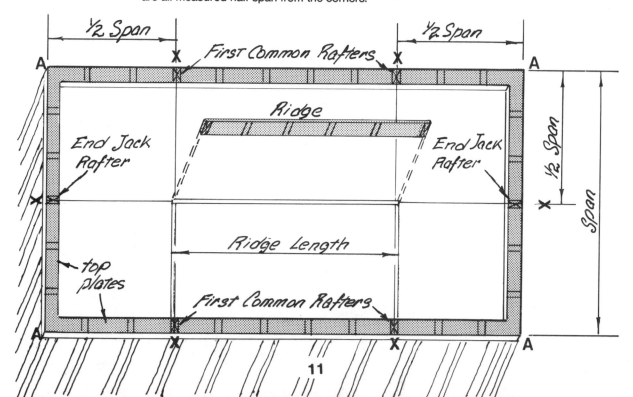

For Hip & Valley Roofs

Top Plates

Step 1 Determine the roof span and measure out from the corners marked "A" the distance A-X. This represents a half span. Similarly, mark positions "Z" on the minor roof plates.

Step 2 Mark out the thickness of the first common rafter and end jack positions. These are located centrally over the half span "X" and "Z" lines. See figs 10 & 11.

Step 3 From these positions, commence setting out rafter spacings towards the building corners. The end spacing may work out shorter. It is good practice to allow an extra jack rafter approximately 150mm-200mm from the corner for added strength and support.

Step 4 Common rafter positions between "X" and "X" along the ridge are set out as equal spacings but not more than that specified.

Ridge The same as ridge for hip roofs. See page 11.

Make a Roof Plan

It is good practice to draw in pencil all the roof members over the house floor plan similar to fig 10 or better still make a 1:50 scale roof plan. When more than one span is incorporated in the roof, such as a main roof, with a smaller extension or offset, identify the members of each roof section, eg. 'common rafter - major roof' and 'common rafter - minor roof' etc.

FIG 10   **Example Roof**

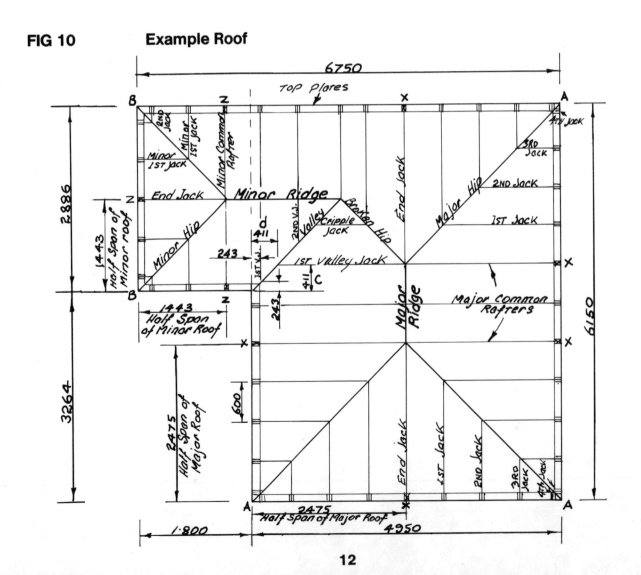

12

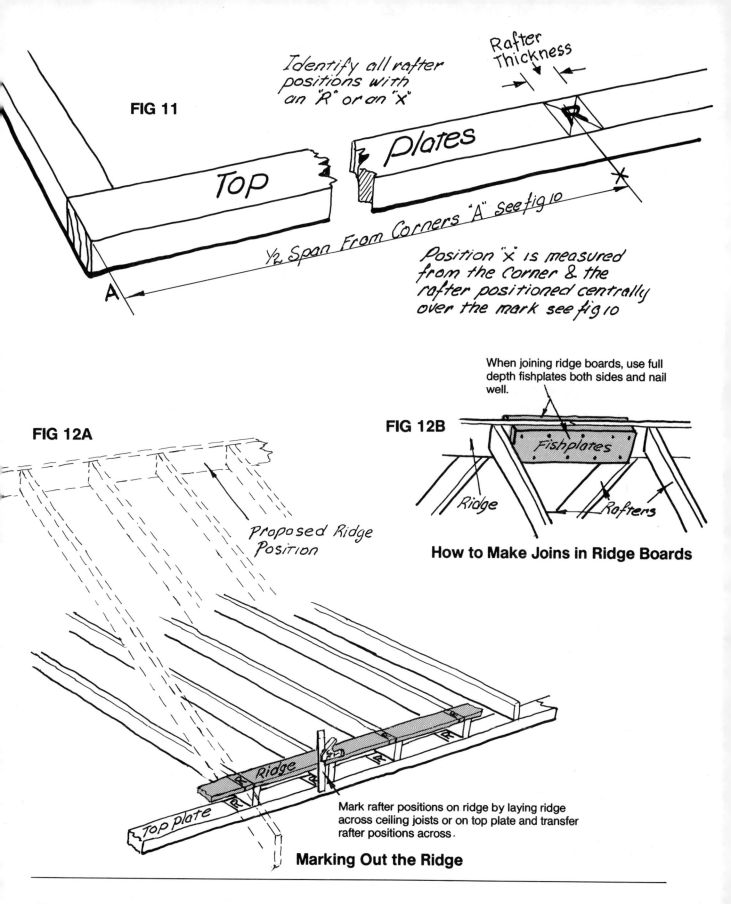

FIG 11

Identify all rafter positions with an "R" or an "x"

Rafter Thickness

Top Plates

R

x

½ Span From Corners "A" see fig 10

A

Position "x" is measured from the corner & the rafter positioned centrally over the mark see fig 10

FIG 12A

Proposed Ridge Position

FIG 12B

When joining ridge boards, use full depth fishplates both sides and nail well.

Fishplates

Ridge

Rafters

How to Make Joins in Ridge Boards

Ridge

Top plate

R

R

Mark rafter positions on ridge by laying ridge across ceiling joists or on top plate and transfer rafter positions across.

Marking Out the Ridge

For Gable Roofs

Top Plates

After marking the end rafter position, set out intermediate rafters at equal spacings. Do not exceed the maximum spacings specified on the plans. Indicate rafter position with an "X" or the letter "R" as in fig 11.

Ridge The same as for Hip Roofs. See page 11. For long ridges commence from one end. Make joins in ridges between rafter spacings as shown in fig 12B.

Marking Out Rafters

Make the Common Rafter Pattern

The following should be prepared at this stage:
1. Lengths obtained from the tables and recorded.
2. Timber sorted and neatly stacked and covered.

3. Tools on hand are: bevel gauge, tape, square, saw, sharp pencil, saw stools
It is normal practice to prepare a single common rafter to use as a pattern from which all others can be marked accurately.

Step 1 Mark the Rafter Length

Select a relatively straight length of rafter timber. From a squared line at one end, measure the geometrical length (given in the tables) along the top edge. Again, square across at this point. It is also helpful whilst measuring to indicate the length required for the eaves overhang. If under purlins are to be used, then its position could be marked on the pattern. By transferring this position to all rafters at this stage, it will eliminate a somewhat troublesome task after the roof has been pitched.

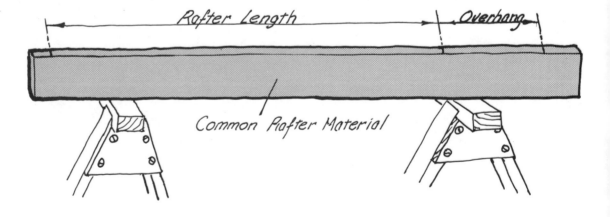

FIG 13

Rafter Length — Overhang

Common Rafter Material

Step 2 Mark the Plumb Cuts

Find on the house plans the degree of pitch specified. Using the bevels from section 7, set the bevel gauge to the rafter plumb cut for the particular degree. This bevel is then transferred to the face of the rafter from the measured points. See fig 14.

FIG 14

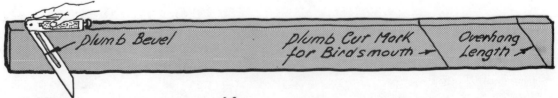

Plumb Bevel — Plumb Cut Mark for Birdsmouth — Overhang Length

Step 3   Mark the Backing Line

Determine the backing line position (usually 2/3 of the rafter width and gauge this line from the top edge. The backing line represents the geometrical (tables) length line. See figs 5 & 16.

FIG 15

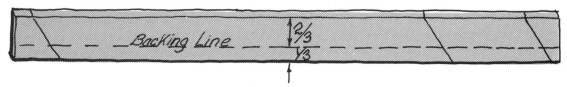

The Birdsmouth Rule

The position of the backing line is dependent upon:

    A. The width of the rafter timbers
    B. The width of the top plate

As a general rule, the backing line should never be positioned less than 2/3rds of the width from the top of the rafter nor should the birdsmouth be any wider than the width of the top plate. See fig 16.

FIG 16

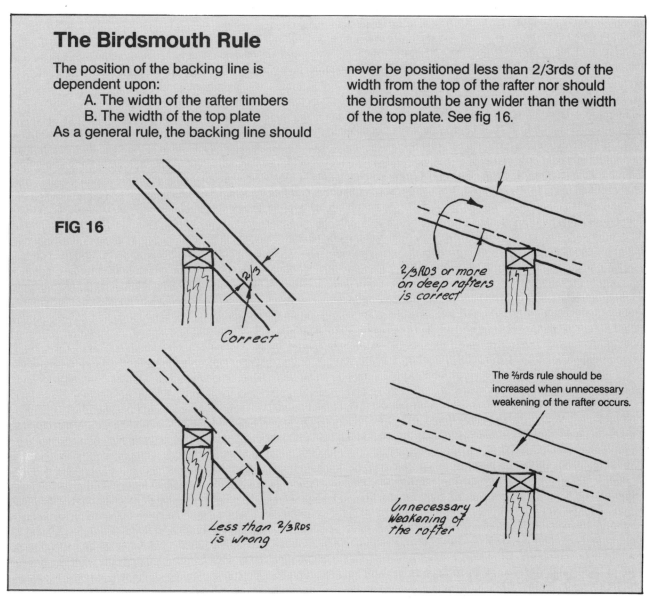

Step 4   Mark the Birdsmouth

Using a bevel guage set to the required rafter seat cut bevel, mark the birdsmouth where the backing line intersects the plumb line. See fig 17.

FIG 17

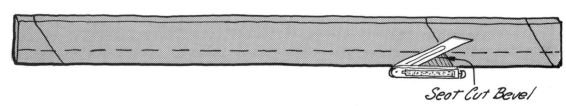

Seat Cut Bevel

Step 5   Mark the Cutting Length

Measure half the ridge board thickness square off the top end plumb line and place a new plumb cut line on this measurement. See fig 18. This reduction in length is necessary because the first plumb line was the geometrical length taken from the tables and actually arrives in the centre of the ridge.

FIG 18

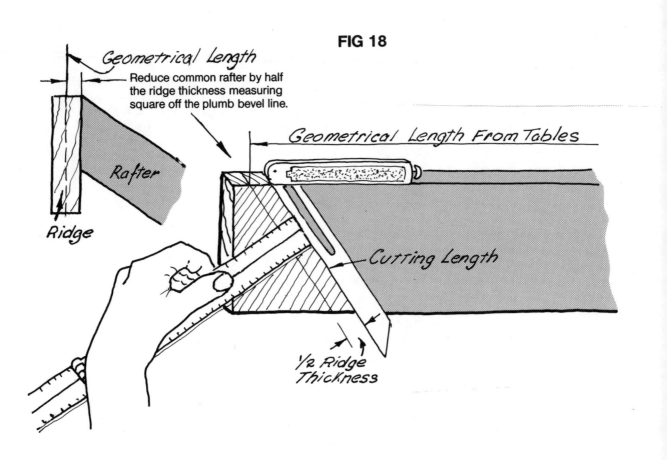

Step 6   Cut the Rafter Pattern

Accurately cut the new top end plumb cut and the birdsmouth. Leave the overhang marked but uncut. This is used as a length gauge only. Its plumb cut mark is not transferred to other rafters. The overhang is best cut after all the rafters are erected. It is then cut off using a chalk line. Mark **pattern** on this rafter clearly to identify it.

FIG 19

Make the Jack Rafter Patterns

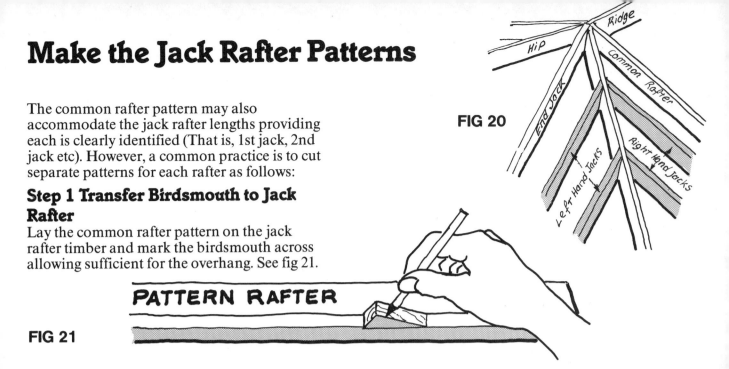

FIG 20

The common rafter pattern may also accommodate the jack rafter lengths providing each is clearly identified (That is, 1st jack, 2nd jack etc). However, a common practice is to cut separate patterns for each rafter as follows:

Step 1 Transfer Birdsmouth to Jack Rafter

Lay the common rafter pattern on the jack rafter timber and mark the birdsmouth across allowing sufficient for the overhang. See fig 21.

FIG 21

Step 2 Mark Geometrical Length of Jack Rafter

Measure the geometrical length of the first jack rafter along the top edge from the birdsmouth and square across. See fig 22. For how to find the length, see section 7.

Step 3 Mark the Edge Cut Bevel

Set a bevel gauge to the jack rafter edge cut (in section 7). Mark this angle across the top edge through the centre of the squared line. See fig 22.

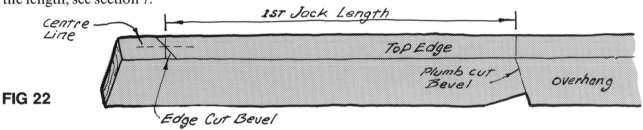

FIG 22

Step 4 Mark the Cutting Length

Reduce the geometrical length by half the thickness of the hip rafter measuring square from the edge bevel. See fig 23.

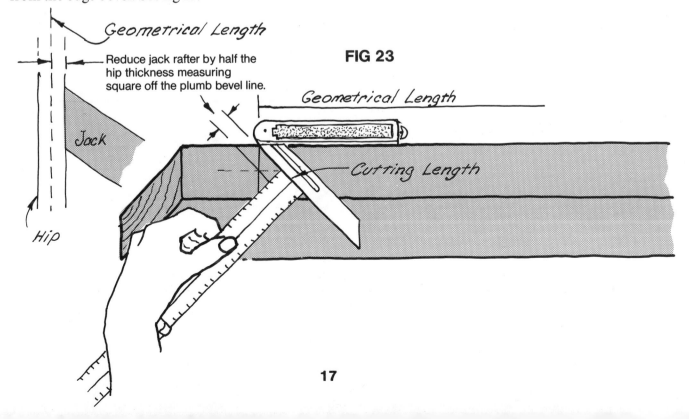

FIG 23

Step 5 Mark the Plumb Cut

Mark the plumb cut across the face from the long point of the edge cut. This will be on the correct face of the rafters for later cutting. See fig 24. (Remember some jacks are left hand and some right. See fig 20.

Note

Figs 24-26 are a continuation of the sequence but for illustrative purposes have been exchanged to left hand jack rafters.

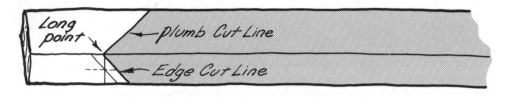

FIG 24

Step 6 Mark Remaining Jack Rafters

The remaining jack rafters can be marked out along the first jack pattern by using equal diminish lengths. See page 39 for explanation of diminish lengths and how to obtain them. Measure the diminish from the long point of the cutting length. This will provide the cutting length of the next and remaining jack rafters. No further reduction for hip thickness necessary. See fig 25-26A & B.

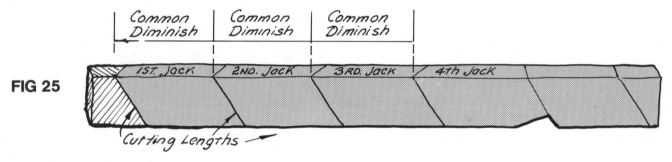

FIG 25

Step 7 Make Separate Jack Patterns

Make a separate pattern for each jack rafter by transferring the relevant marks across from the master pattern.

FIG 26A

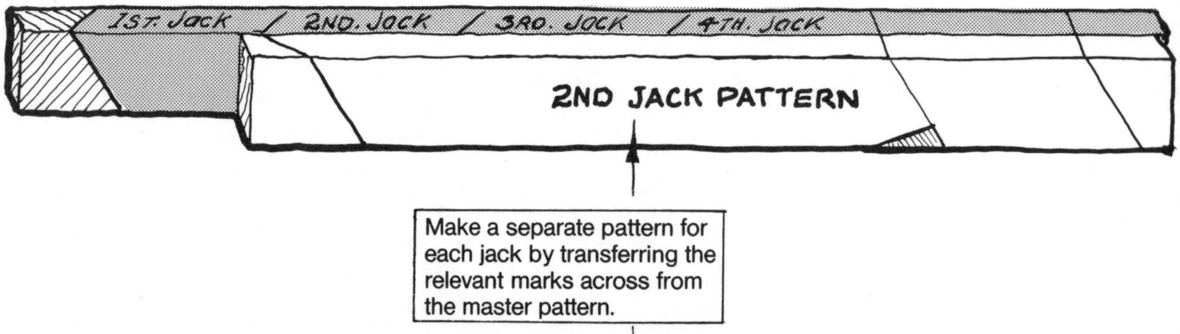

2ND JACK PATTERN

Make a separate pattern for each jack by transferring the relevant marks across from the master pattern.

FIG 26B

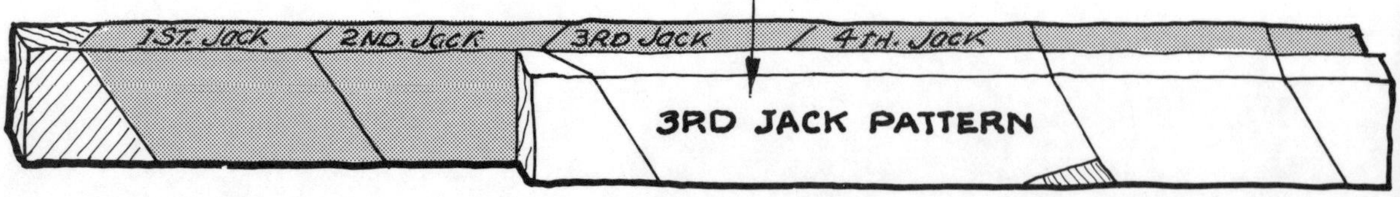

3RD JACK PATTERN

Valley Jack Rafters

Valley jacks do not have birdsmouths and are usually measured from the top end plumb cut. The method used to obtain these lengths is found in sections 5 & 7 They will be reduced to cutting lengths by half the thickness of the valley rafter at their lower end and half the thickness of the ridge at their top end. See figs 27A & B.

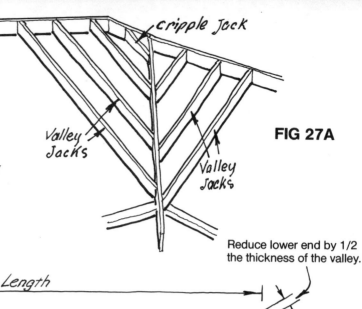

FIG 27A

Reduce upper end by 1/2 the thickness of the ridge.

FIG 27B

Reduce lower end by 1/2 the thickness of the valley.

Geometrical Length

Cutting Length   Cutting Length

End Jack Rafter

Although this rafter has the same geometrical length as the common rafter, its cutting length may be different. When the ridge thickness is the same as the common rafter thickness, then cutting lengths will be identical. When the ridge is thinner (as it usually is), the length of the end jack will need to be reduced. The reduction is half the thickness of the common rafter measuring square off the plumb cut line. See fig 28.

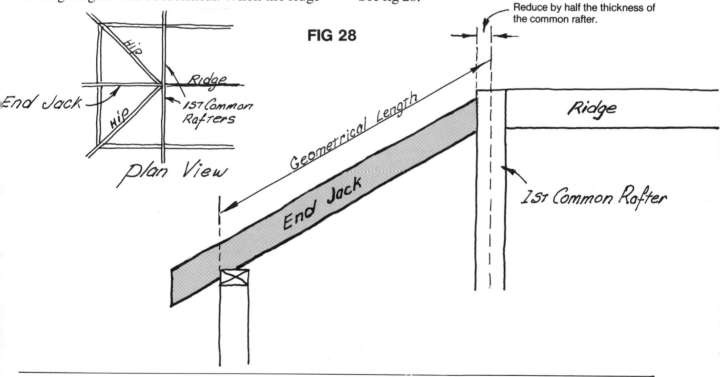

FIG 28

Reduce by half the thickness of the common rafter.

Hip & Valley Rafters

The length of hip and valley rafters are best obtained by actual sight measurement. This procedure is explained in Section 5. However, to find hip and valley lengths from the tables for estimating purposes see page 39.

4

Cutting Out

Working close to the stack of timber will reduce handling time and effort. Set up saw stools with a clear working space around them.

Common Rafters

Step 1 Lay out a number of timber lengths with their rounds to the top edge. Lay the pattern rafter over each rafter allowing sufficient overhang length. Ensure the top edges of the pattern align with uncut rafter at the 2 points marked X in fig 29. Commence tracing the birdsmouth and plumb cuts across. See fig 30. Use a sharp pencil for accuracy.

Step 2 When all rafters on the stools have been marked out, commence cutting them. The top plumb cut may be cut with a hand or power saw. The birdsmouth may be partly cut with a power saw and then finished off with a hand saw. It is preferable to cut overhang ends to a chalk line after all rafters have been erected.

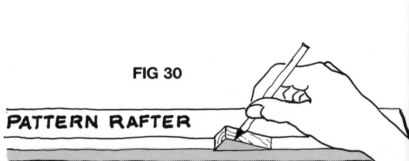

FIG 29

When transferring birdsmouth and plumb cuts across from pattern rafter, the top edges should be kept flush at the X points.

FIG 30

PATTERN RAFTER

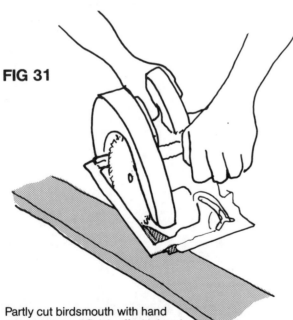

FIG 31

Partly cut birdsmouth with hand power saw and finish off with hand saw. Alternatively, set the radial arm saw to the depth and bevel of the birdsmouth and cut 1 or more at the same time.

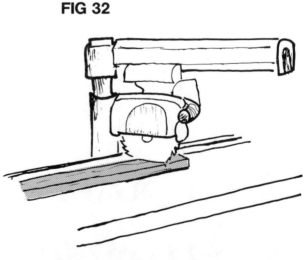

FIG 32

Rafters are often cut to length on a radial arm saw.

Jack Rafters

Lay out jack rafters with rounds to the top and bows to the left for left handed jacks and to the right for right handed. See fig 33. Align the edges of the jack pattern rafters over each jack the same as in fig 29. When cutting the top end of jack rafters, set the base plate of the power saw to 45 degrees and cut along the plumb line. This will produce the required angle across the edge. See figs 34A & B and 35.
Valley jacks and cripple jacks are cut in the same manner.
Mark each rafter with lumber crayon to identify its position in the roof.

Hip, Broken Hip & Valley Rafters

Hip, broken hip and valley rafters can be measured on site and these lengths marked out as on pages 24-29. For shortening, see pages 41 & 42. The cuts are made using the methods described above.

FIG 33

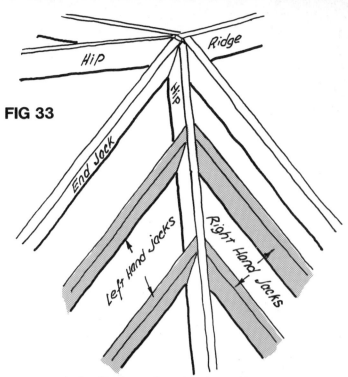

Jack rafters are selected and cut with bows left and right to fit their left and right hand positions.

FIG 34B

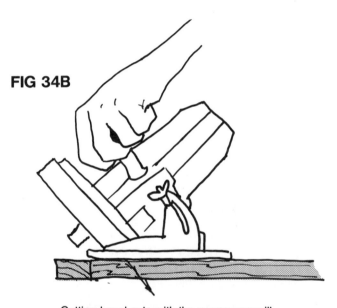

Cutting bevel cuts with the power saw will automatically give the edge bevel.

FIG 34A

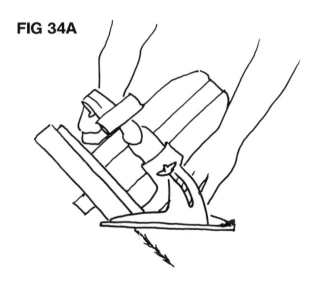

When cutting hips and hip jacks to length set the power saw base to 45 degrees.

FIG 35

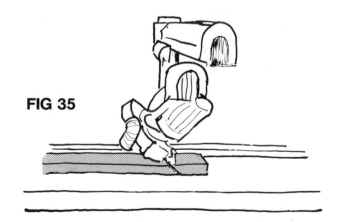

5

Erecting the Roof

How to Erect the Roof

FIG 36

At this stage, all wall frames should be erected, plumbed and top plates straightened and braced. Ceiling joists can be fixed in position adjacent to rafter positions. Hanging and strutting beams are then fixed in position. Planks to provide a working platform are hoisted over the ceiling joists. The rafters are then set out on the ridge as on page 13 and the ridge cut to length.

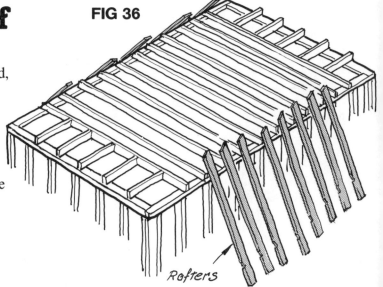

Rafters

Erecting Common Rafters & Ridges

Step 1 Stand all cut rafters on their ends in approximate positions against external walls ready for use. See fig 36.

Step 2 Raise one pair of opposing rafters at each end of the ridge nailing their lower ends into position. Tack the pairs together at the top temporarily and attach temporary braces to support them plumb. See fig 37.

FIG 37

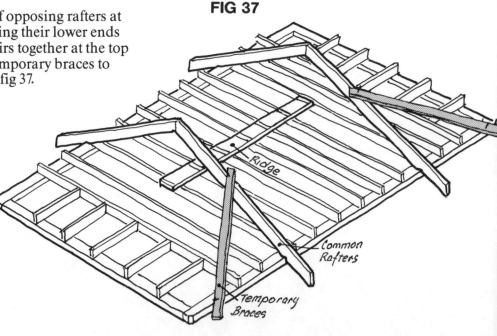

Ridge

Common Rafters

Temporary Braces

22

Step 3 Raise the ridge into position between the rafters and fix. See fig 38. Some tradesmen attach a temporary brace from the ridge as in fig 39 and dispense with the other temporary braces in fig 37.

FIG 38

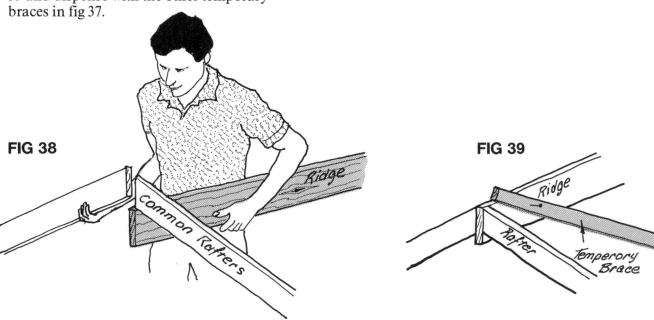

FIG 39

On a Gable Roof
The end pairs of rafters are plumbed over the wall frames with a level or plumb bob and temporarily braced. The remaining rafters are installed and then permanent braces attached.

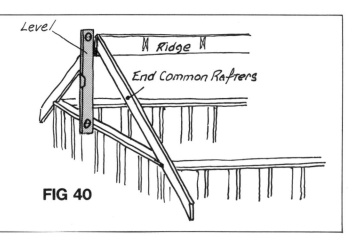

FIG 40

Step 4 Raise the end jacks to provide the bracing for the rafters. See fig 41. Then attach the remaining rafters in pairs straightening the ridge at the same time. Align the top corners of the end jacks with the edges of the rafters as in fig 42.

FIG 41

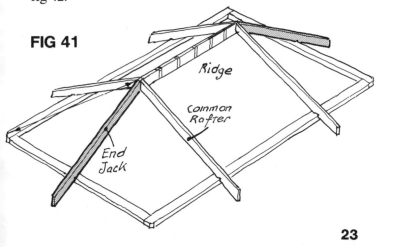

FIG 42

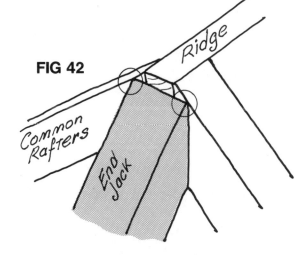

Erecting Hip Rafters

Step 1 Cut away the corner of the top plate at 45 degrees to allow a snug fit for the birdsmouth. See fig 43.

Step 2 Prepare the hip by marking the birdsmouth first, allowing sufficient for the overhang. The hip is longer than the common rafters because it is on the diagonal.

Note To set the top of the hip rafter in line with the top of the common rafters the backing line is positioned at the same distance down from the top edge. Then the plumb cut line on the birdsmouth is adjusted to fit into the sawn off corner of the top plate. This new plumb cut line is made by measuring along the seat cut line a distance of half the thickness of the hip. The seat cut line is not altered. This means that this new birdsmouth will be below the backing line. See fig 44

Step 3 To find the length of the hip, hold a tape between the two measuring points as illustrated in fig 45A, B, & C.

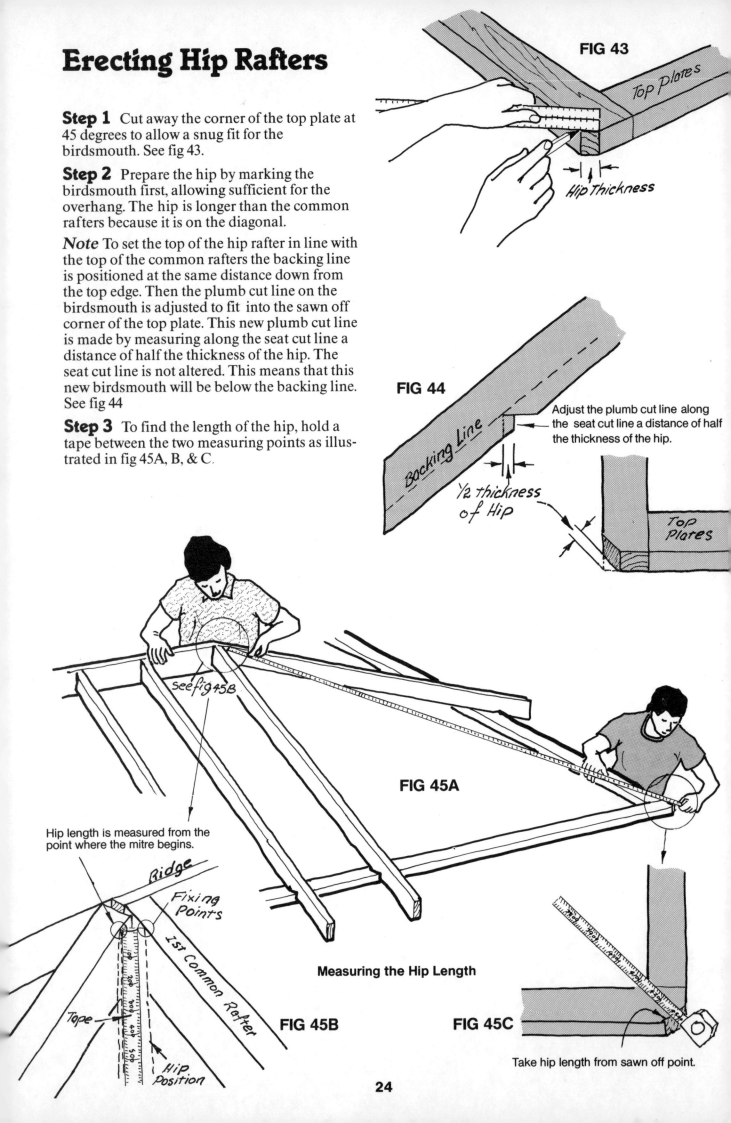

FIG 43

Top Plates

Hip Thickness

FIG 44

Backing Line

½ thickness of Hip

Adjust the plumb cut line along the seat cut line a distance of half the thickness of the hip.

Top Plates

see fig 45B

FIG 45A

Hip length is measured from the point where the mitre begins.

Ridge

Fixing Points

1st Common Rafter

Tape

Hip Position

FIG 45B

Measuring the Hip Length

FIG 45C

Take hip length from sawn off point.

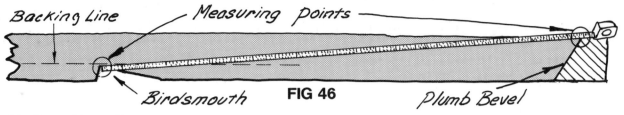

Backing Line — Measuring points

Birdsmouth

FIG 46

Plumb Bevel

Backing line on hips are the same
distance down from the top edge as
common rafters.

Edge cut lines are only used as a guide when
hand sawing and are not necessary when using
a power saw.

Step 4 Apply the measured length to the hip
holding the end of the tape at the corner of the
birdsmouth, then across the face until the
measured length intersects with top edge. The
hip plumb cut bevel is marked at this point
across each face. See fig 46. The hip plumb cut
bevel will be found in section 7.

Step 5 With a bevel gauge set to the hip edge
cut bevel, mark the top edge from both faces.
See fig 47. If using a power saw, this step is
unnecessary as setting the base of the saw at
45 degrees and cutting along the plumb lines on
each face will result in the correct angle.

Step 6 Raise the rafter into position and fix
with top edges intersecting firmly with the fixing
points. See fig 45B.

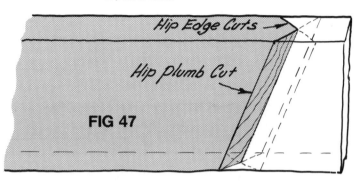

Hip Edge Cuts

Hip Plumb Cut

FIG 47

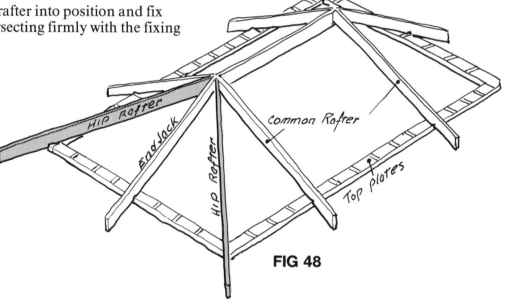

Hip Rafter

End Jack

Hip Rafter

common Rafter

Top plates

FIG 48

Erecting Jack Rafters

Jack rafters are fixed in pairs on each side of the
hip. Commence with the centre pair at the same
time straightening the hip to a string line. See fig
49. For finding the lengths of jack rafters see
page 41.

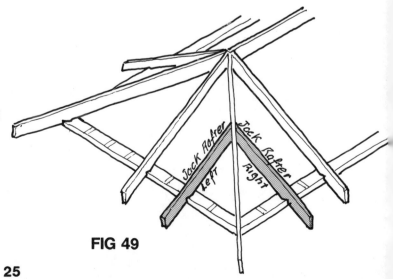

Jack Rafter Left

Jack Rafter Right

FIG 49

Erecting Broken Hip Rafters

It can be seen from fig 52 that length measurements for the broken hip is unnecessary because its lower end can simply be cut to overhang past its fixing point. All that is required is the cut off point for the minor ridge against which the broken hip is fixed.

However, for estimating purposes, the length can be found by deducting the geometrical lengths of the hip rafter in the minor roof from the length of the hip in the major roof. This results in the length of the broken hip.

Step 1 Stretch a line from the centre of the major ridge, hip and common rafter intersection to point A on the wall plate where the major roof span meets the minor. See fig 50B. At this lower point the string should be attached at the common height of the rafters. Do this by either inserting a temporary rafter as illustrated in fig 50A or by using packing blocks.

Note Ensure the string is positioned centrally over the point where the major and minor roofs meet and plumb off the outside edge of the wall plate.

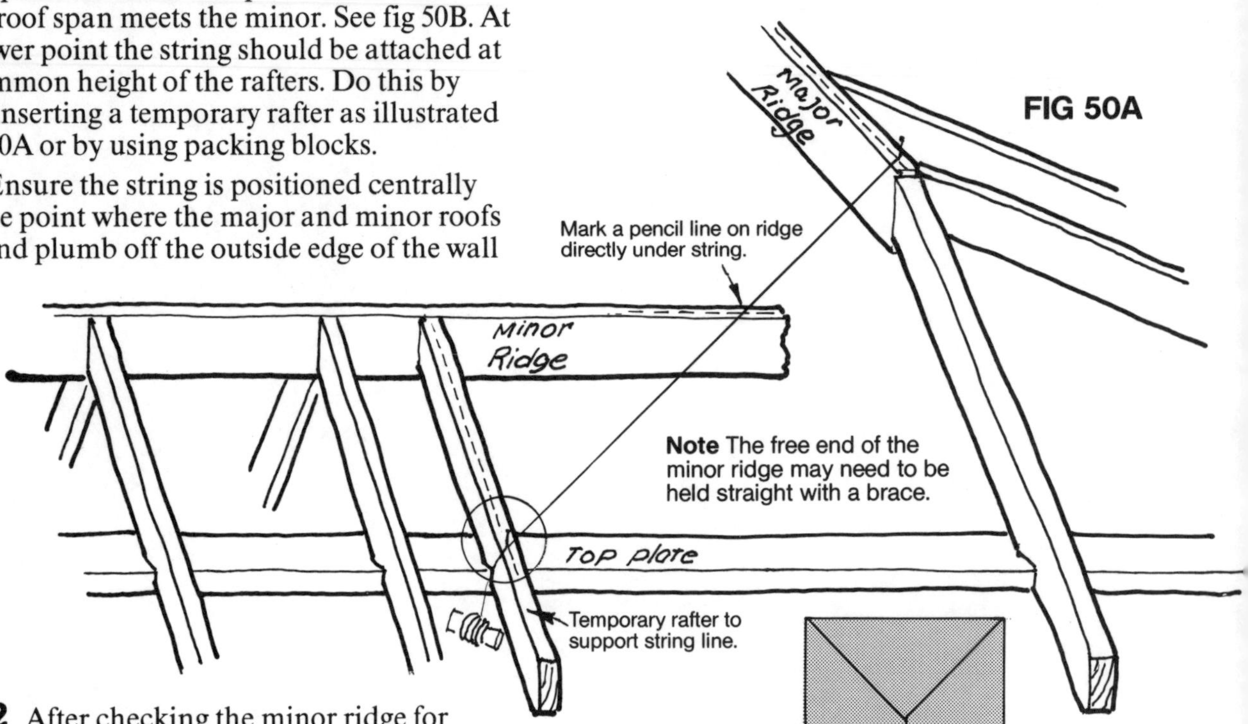

FIG 50A

Mark a pencil line on ridge directly under string.

Minor Ridge

Note The free end of the minor ridge may need to be held straight with a brace.

Top plate

Temporary rafter to support string line.

Step 2 After checking the minor ridge for straightness, scribe a line along the centre of its top edge. This free end of the ridge may need to be held straight with a brace.

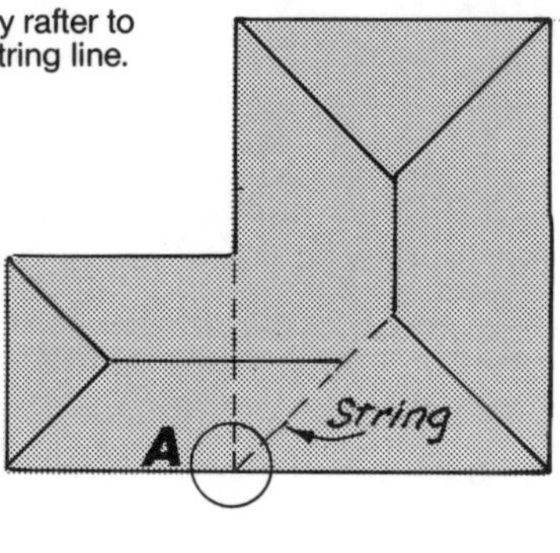

Step 3 Mark a line on the top edge of the minor ridge directly under the string. This line should be at 45 degrees. This line represents the centre line of the broken hip, therefore, to accommodate the broken hip, the ridge must be reduced from this line by half the thickness of the broken hip. This reduction is measured square off the string line mark. See figs 51A and B. The 90 degree plumb line can also be marked.

A   String   FIG 50B

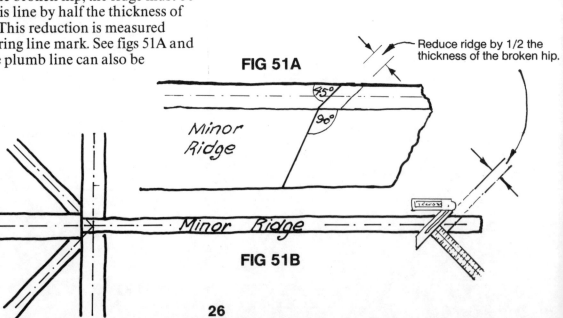

FIG 51A

Reduce ridge by 1/2 the thickness of the broken hip.

45°

90°

Minor Ridge

Minor Ridge

FIG 51B

26

Step 4 The ridge can now be cut to these marks.

Step 5 Prepare the top cuts of the broken hip in the same manner as a full hip. See fig 47 page 25.

Step 6 Fix the broken hip into position as shown in fig 52. The tail end may be cut flush with the face of the ridge or the waste left as shown. When nailing the lower end of the broken hip to the minor ridge, ensure the top edges are in alignment. See figs 53A & B.

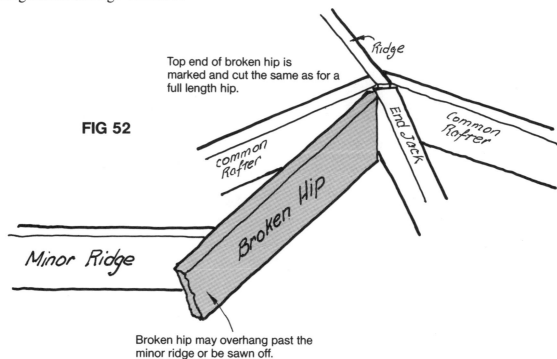

Top end of broken hip is marked and cut the same as for a full length hip.

FIG 52

Broken hip may overhang past the minor ridge or be sawn off.

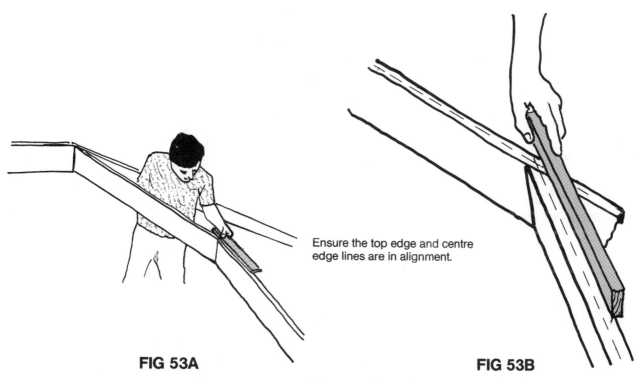

Ensure the top edge and centre edge lines are in alignment.

FIG 53A

FIG 53B

Erecting Valley Rafters

Step 1 Mark lines down the centre of the broken hip and minor ridge until they intersect as in figs 54A & B. Then square a line through this intersection at 90 degrees off the broken hip (or at 45 degrees off the minor ridge).

Step 2 Measure the length of the valley, holding the tape on the internal corner of the top plates and up to the measuring point just marked. See fig 55.
Note For double checking, remember the tables length of the valley rafter is the same as the hip in the minor roof.

Step 3 Scribe the backing line on the valley rafter ensuring it is the same common distance down from the top edge as all the other rafters. Then mark the birdsmouth using the hip seat and plumb cut bevels. Do not cut at this stage.

Step 4 Apply the measured length to the face of the rafter measuring from the corner of the birdsmouth to the top edge. Refer to similar in fig 46 page 25.

Step 5 Square a bevel at 90 degrees across the edge from the measured point. Through this line mark the centre of the valley. Then through the intersection of these lines, mark the hip edge bevel. On the face mark the hip plumb cut bevel and saw through this line. See fig 56A

Step 6 Measure the distance A in fig 56B and transfer this measurement to the edge cut on the valley. Square this line across at 90 degrees and remove this end portion.

Follow the sequence 1 to 7 for marking and cutting the valley.

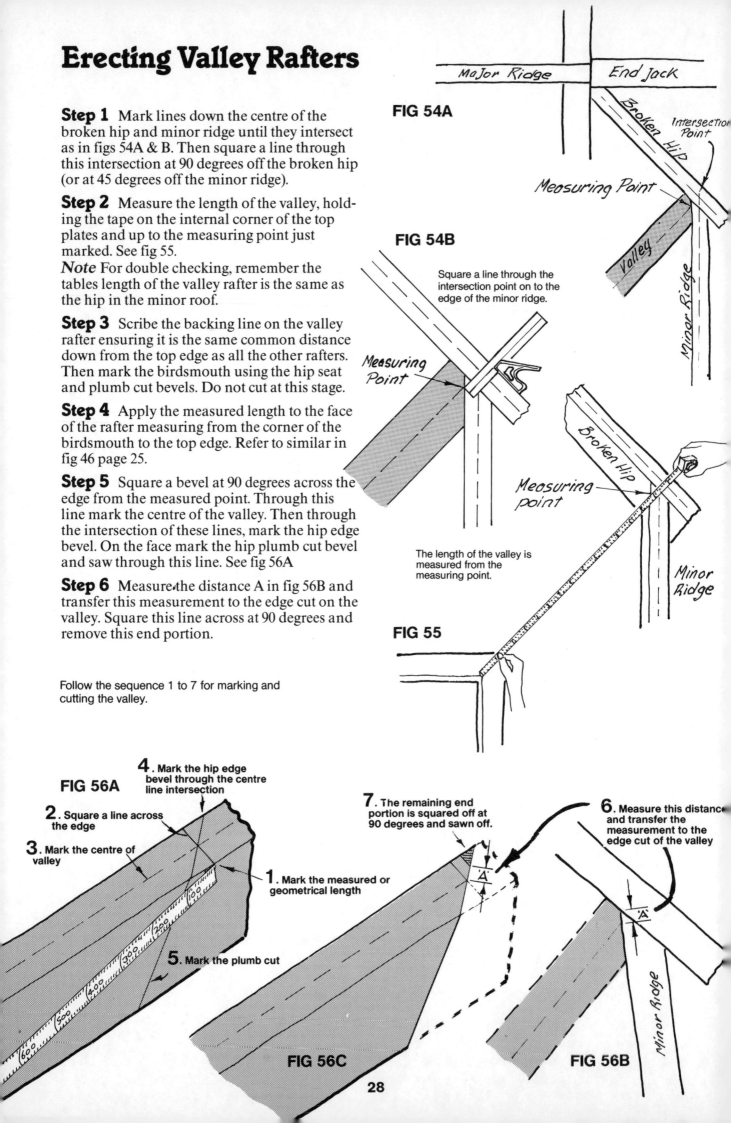

FIG 54A

Major Ridge End Jack Broken Hip Intersection Point Measuring Point Valley Minor Ridge

FIG 54B

Square a line through the intersection point on to the edge of the minor ridge.

Measuring Point

FIG 55

Broken Hip Measuring point Minor Ridge

The length of the valley is measured from the measuring point.

FIG 56A

4. Mark the hip edge bevel through the centre line intersection

2. Square a line across the edge

3. Mark the centre of valley

1. Mark the measured or geometrical length

5. Mark the plumb cut

FIG 56C

7. The remaining end portion is squared off at 90 degrees and sawn off.

6. Measure this distance and transfer the measurement to the edge cut of the valley

'A'

'A'

Minor Ridge

FIG 56B

28

Step 7 Figures 57A & B show an additional birdsmouth plumb line below the one marked in step 3. The reason for this is to enable the valley to fit into the internal corner. Mark this new line half the thickness of the valley down from the original plumb line. Then on the underneath edge, mark hip edge cut bevels to intersect in the centre as in fig 57B.

Step 8 Cut the rafter and fix into position aligning the top edge centre line with the measuring point as in figs 54A & B.

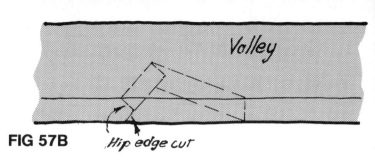

FIG 57B

Hip edge cut

FIG 58

Valley

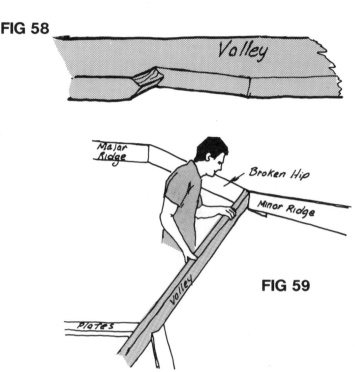

FIG 59

Major Ridge

Broken Hip

Minor Ridge

Valley

Plates

FIG 57A

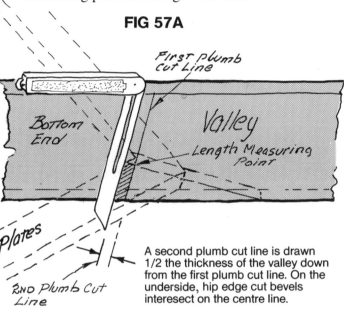

First plumb Cut Line

Bottom End

Valley

Length Measuring Point

Plates

2ND Plumb Cut Line

A second plumb cut line is drawn 1/2 the thickness of the valley down from the first plumb cut line. On the underside, hip edge cut bevels interesect on the centre line.

Erecting Valley Rafters

(When Intersecting Two Equal Span Roofs)

Where both spans of a hip and valley roof are equal, the geometrical length of the valley will be the same as that of the hip. See fig 60. Cutting Lengths are Found as Follows:

Step 1 Tape the length of the valley from the internal corner of the top plate to the internal corner intersection of the ridges. See fig 61.

Step 2 Mark the birdsmouth using hip seat and plumb cuts. Do not cut at this stage.

Step 3 Apply the measured length to the face of the rafter from the corner of the birdsmouth to the top edge as for hips in fig 46 page 25, except that the measurement for the top end is taken to the long point as arrowed in fig 61.

Step 4 Adjust the birdsmouth position as in step 7 above. Then cut and fix into position.

FIG 60

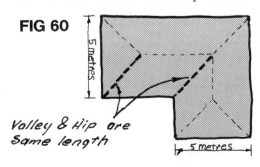

Valley & Hip are Same length

5 metres

5 metres

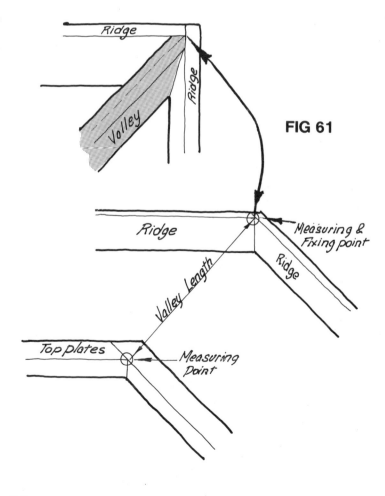

Ridge

Valley

Ridge

FIG 61

Ridge

Ridge

Measuring & Fixing point

Valley Length

Top plates

Measuring Point

29

Erecting Valley Jack Rafters & Cripple Jacks

Valley jacks are spaced apart at the same spacings specified for all other rafters. They are cut and fitted commencing with the longest. Each subsequent jack is reduced in length by an equal amount. This is termed the 'common diminish'. The length of valley jacks can be obtained by finding the run and applying the tables as explained on page 40 (being the method most commonly used) or by on site measurement as explained in step 2 below.

Steps to Installing Valley Jacks

Step 1 Mark the jack spacings along the ridge board.

Step 2 Mark the position for the first or longest jack on both sides of the valley as in fig 62. Then the length of the longest jacks can be obtained by using the method described on page 40 or by measuring on site as in figs 62 & 63. When measuring on site, tape the length of the longest jacks as in fig 62 holding the tape 10mm above the jack.

Step 3 Mark out a pattern for the longest valley jack. See figs 27 A.&B. page 19.

Step 4 On the same pattern, mark the lengths of the remaining jacks. To find the amount to diminish each one. See 'diminish' under **The Jack Rafter** page 39.

Step 5 The edge and face cut bevels are obtained from section 7 and transferred to each jack rafter.

Step 6 Jacks can now be cut to length and installed. Fix valley jacks in pairs. Ensure the valley is maintained in straight alignment. See figs 64 & 79

Cripple Jacks

Cripple jacks fit between the broken hip and valley. The jack rafter edge cut bevel is used on both ends and the hip plumb cut is used on the face, both ends. The length can be taped on site as the long jack was in fig 62 or measured using the tables. See page 40.

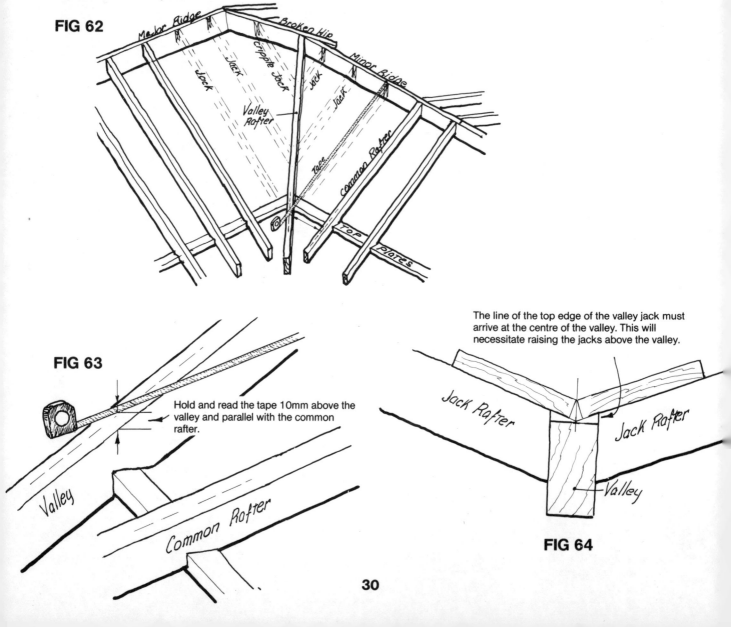

FIG 62

FIG 63

Hold and read the tape 10mm above the valley and parallel with the common rafter.

The line of the top edge of the valley jack must arrive at the centre of the valley. This will necessitate raising the jacks above the valley.

FIG 64

6

Miscellaneous Details

Underpurlins: support the centre of rafters thus allowing smaller sized rafters to be used. They should be positioned as close as possible to the mid span of the rafter provided adequate strutting can be arranged. This may influence its positioning.

Edge and face cut bevels for underpurlins are provided in section 7. These bevels allow for the underpurlins to be mitred at hip and valley intersections. Joins in underpurlins should be made over a strut. See fig 66C. Under purlins are usually installed as in fig 66A but rafters can be birdsmouthed to receive them as in fig 66B.

Collar Ties: Generally for roofs in excess of 10 degrees slope and when the span of the rafters need support from the underpurlins, collar ties are used to tie rafters together at their midway section. They assist in the even distribution of forces applied to the roof structure.

Collar ties are positioned above underpurlins and bolted with a 10mm bolt to each alternate pair of rafters which coincide with a roof strut.

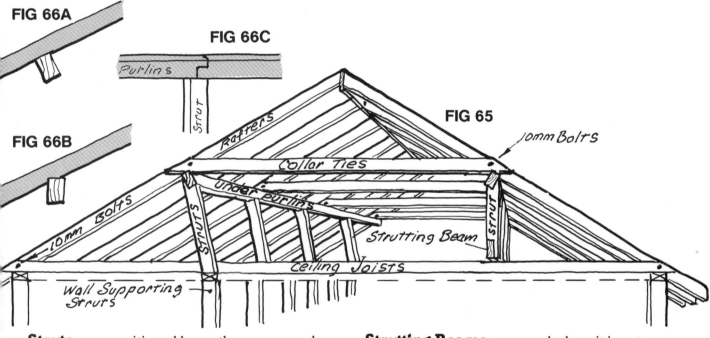

FIG 66A

FIG 66C

FIG 66B

FIG 65

Struts: are positioned beneath every second rafter and are placed at angles up to 30 degrees in any direction. Where the angle must exceed 30 degrees but not more than 45 degrees, the strut is opposed by another strut at the same angle. See fig 71. Struts transfer roof loads to the wall framing. Where struts can't be secured directly on to a wall frame, strutting beams are used as in fig 67 underpurlins may be strutted from walls running parallel or at right angles. See figs 68 & 69.

Strutting Beams: are used where it is not possible to strutt off partitions. Each end of the beam is blocked up above ceiling joists 25mm to allow the beam to flex without transferring roof loads to the ceiling joists. For this reason, ceiling joists should never be hung from strutting beams.

Where a beam is supported on an external wall, its end may need to be cut to the angle of the rafter as in fig 70.

FIG 67

FIG 68

FIG 69

FIG 70

Cont

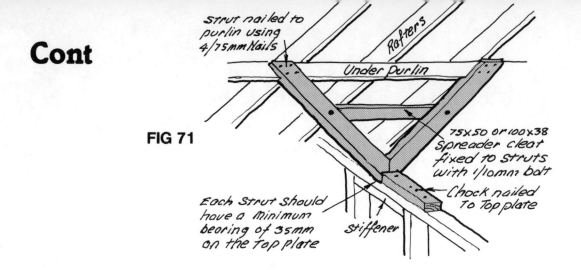

FIG 71

Strut nailed to purlin using 4/75mm Nails

Rafters

Under Purlin

75x50 or 100x38 Spreader cleat fixed to struts with 1/10mm bolt

Chock nailed to Top plate

Each Strut should have a minimum bearing of 35mm on the Top plate

Stiffener

How to Make Struts

When a row of strutting is required with the same bevels, make a pattern of the top and bottom ends.

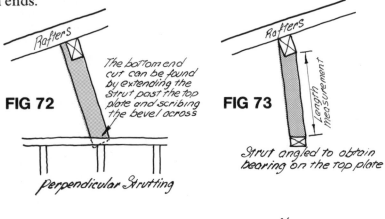

FIG 72

Rafters

The bottom end cut can be found by extending the strut past the top plate and scribing the bevel across

Perpendicular Strutting

FIG 73

Rafters

Length measurement

Strut angled to obtain bearing on the top plate

FIG 74

Rafters

Length measurement

Vertical Strutting from a Strutting beam

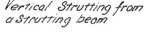

Making the Top End Cut

Step 1 Hold strut or pattern material alongside the under purlin at the top end and plate or strutting beam at the bottom. Then using a rule or straight edge, continue the line of the underpurlin across to the strut as in fig 75.

Step 2 Obtain the vertical line by holding a square at right angles to the line marked in step 1. See fig 76.

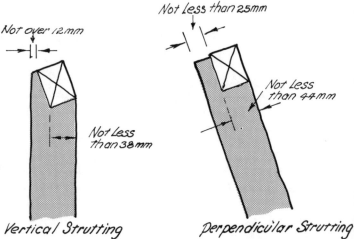

Not over 12mm

Not Less than 38mm

Vertical Strutting

Not Less than 25mm

Not Less than 44mm

Perpendicular Strutting

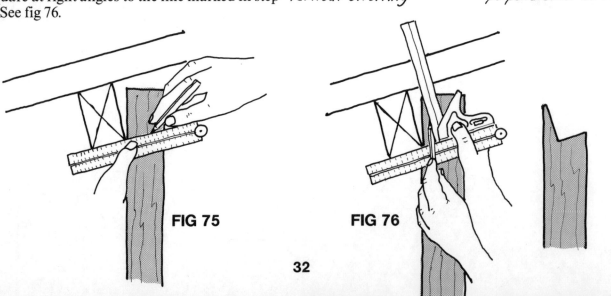

FIG 75

FIG 76

Making the Bottom End Cut

Step 1 Hold the strut on the side of the top plate and set the adjustable bevel to the required angle. See fig 77.

Step 2 Take a measurement between two common points from the under purlin down to the top plate or beam. See figs 73 & 74. Transfer this measurement to the strut and apply the bevel as in fig 78.

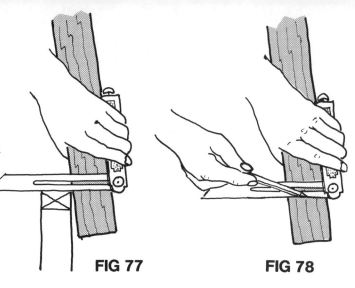

FIG 77   **FIG 78**

Aligning Members

All roof surfaces must be kept as straight as possible. To achieve correct alignment, apply a straightedge during the fixing of rafters. Ensure the straightedge is touching on all those points arrowed in the illustration.

FIG 79

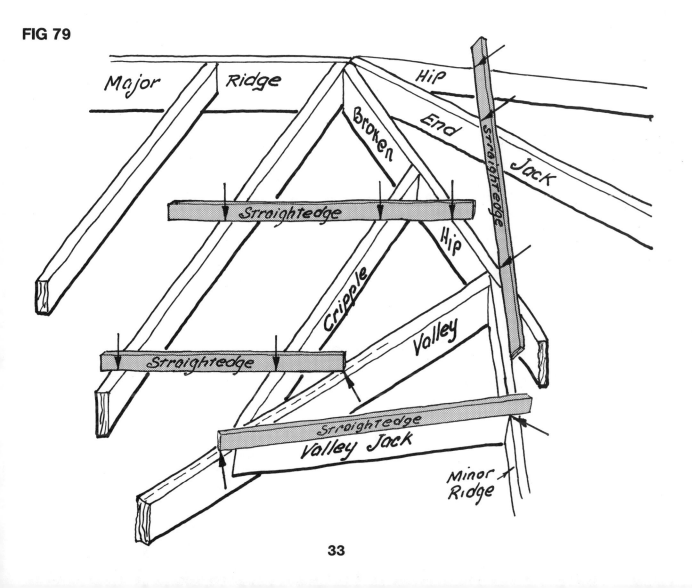

Roof Bracing & Tie Down

Bracing

Due to its design, a hipped roof is self bracing and does not require further bracing. A gable roof, however, does require bracing.

The most commonly applied roof bracing is either perforated V crimped speed brace (the easiest to apply) or perforated flat steel strap which requires tensioning with patented tensioners prior to intermediate fixing.

House plans or specifications will specify the type, quantity and placing of bracing. Metal bracing is attached to the top edges of rafters prior to batten fixing. The two bracing types mentioned above are tension braces and therefore should be applied in opposing pairs as in fig 80.

When attaching speed brace, it should be checked for straightness. Two 30mm x 3.15mm flat head nails are required at each crossing. See fig 81 . At overlapping joins, three nails are driven through common holes as in fig 82. At the top end, the brace is bent and turned over the rafter and three nails driven as in fig 83. At the lower end, the brace is turned down and either bent under the top plate and six nails driven or turned down the studs and six nails driven. See figs 84A & B. Manufacturer's instruction pamphlets are available and should take precedence over the information provided here.

Tying Down

As roofs are subject to a high degree of wind turbulence at times, the roofing members must not only be fixed securely but tied down to resist uplift.

The plans and specifications should specify the tie down requirements. Tie down devices commonly applied are triple or multi grips, cyclone straps and nailing plates. Ensure the correct number of nails are used on triple or multi grips and cyclone straps. When using bolts, ensure the nuts are tightened prior to attaching claddings.

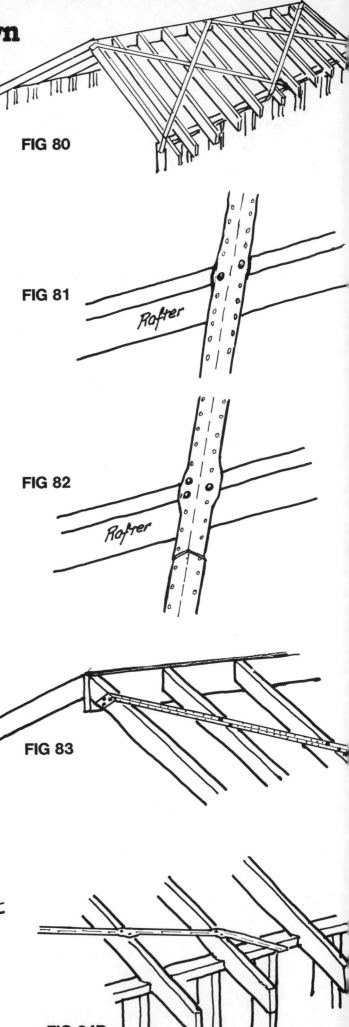

FIG 80

FIG 81

Rafter

FIG 82

Rafter

FIG 83

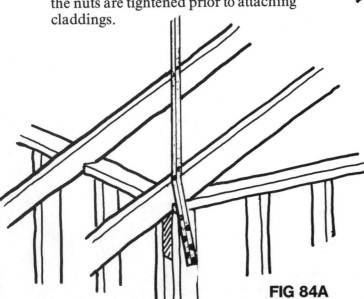

FIG 84A

FIG 84B

Ceiling Joists & Hanging Beams

Ceiling joists not only support ceiling linings but also act as a tie between the feet of opposing pairs of rafters and stiffening to the top plates of wall frames. See fig 85A. Joist ends should be bolted to each alternate pairs of rafters using 10mm bolts as in fig 85B.

Joists beside partitions support cornice mouldings and are positioned according to fig 86.

Ceiling joists and rafter positions are marked out on the top plates at the same time but the ceiling joists are fixed in position prior to any roof members being attached.

Where ceiling joists need to be joined in their length, they should be lapped at least 3 times their depth or butted and cleated both sides. All joins should be made over a supporting wall or beam. Where internal walls run parallel to joists, nogging is fixed between the joists to provide fixing for the wall top plate. See fig 87.

At the ends of a hip roof, the end joist is set back in order not to restrict the fixing of the jack rafters and also to enable short trimmers to be installed to tie the jack rafters back to the ceiling frame. See fig 88.

Ceiling Binders

Two ceiling binders 75mm x 50mm are fixed across the top of ceiling joists and laid on the flat. Where the building width exceeds 9m, three binders are applied evenly spaced. See fig 89A. In some States, the ends are bolted as in fig 89B. Strutting beams, hanging beams or purlins may be used as binders.

Hanging Beams

Hanging beams provide support for ceiling joists where the span between walls is too great for the joist size. They carry the load of the ceiling only and clearance must be provided between roof carrying members to ensure their load is not imposed on the ceiling.

Ceiling joists are hung from hanging beams by either metal straps or 38mm x 38mm timber. At external walls hanging beams are cut, supported and fixed as in fig 88.

FIG 85 A

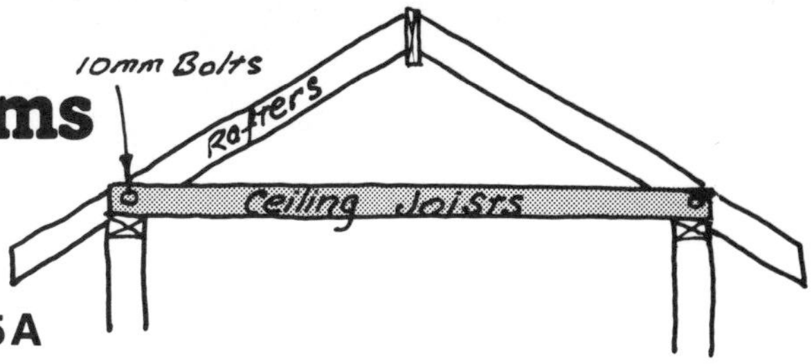

FIG 85B

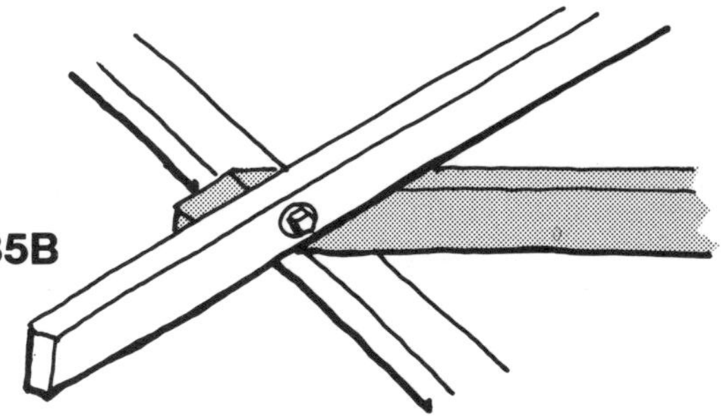

FIG 86 Side A   Side B

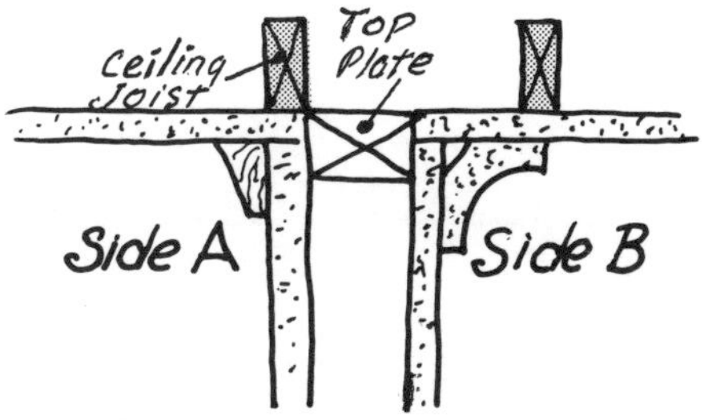

When small ceiling cornice or scosias are applied, the edge ceiling joist is positioned close to the top plate. See side A. When larger cornices are applied, the edge ceiling joist is positioned to support the cornice edge. See side B.

FIG 87

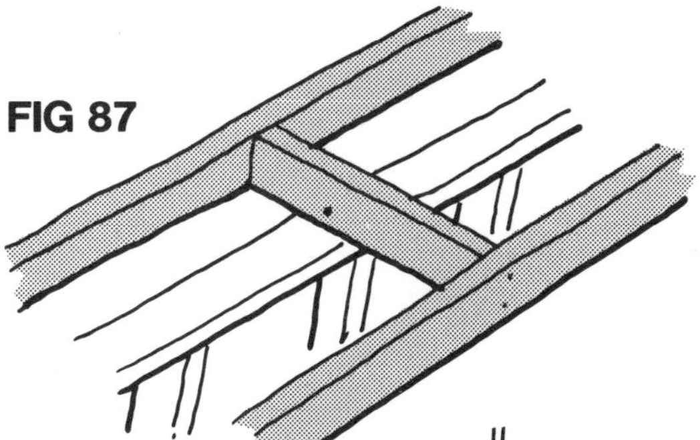

FIG 88

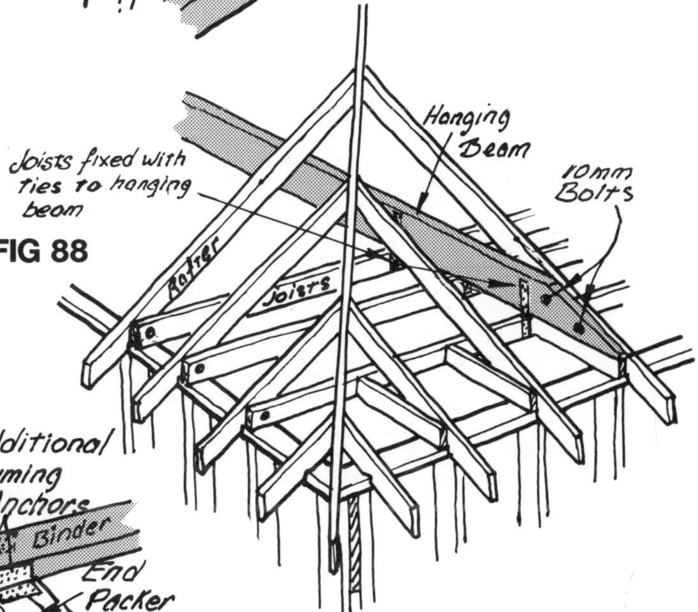

FIG 89A

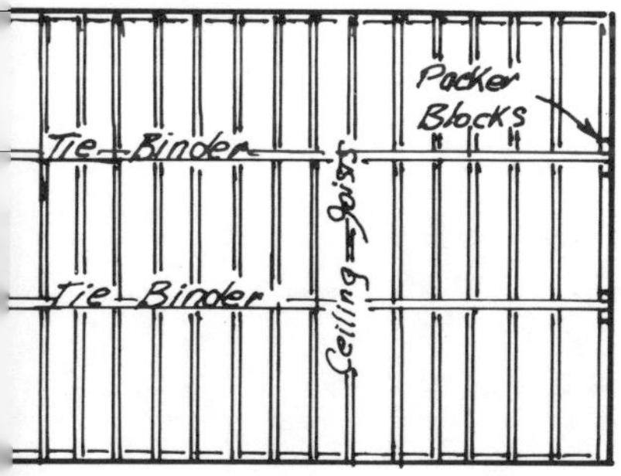

FIG 89B

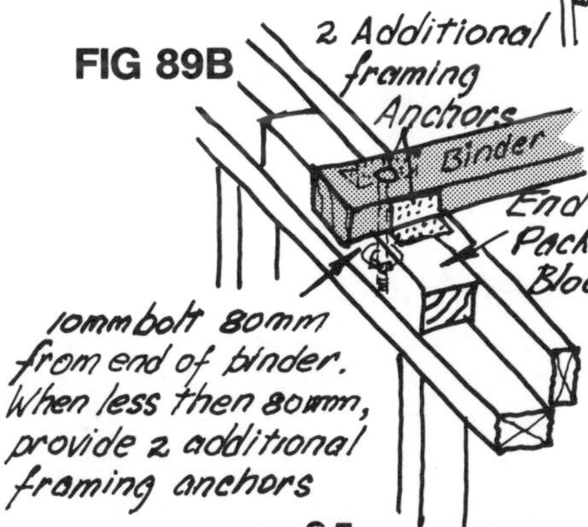

10mm bolt 80mm from end of binder. When less then 80mm, provide 2 additional framing anchors

Cathedral Ceiling Roofs

Cathedral ceilings are an architectural feature which increases the ceiling height and are commonly associated with exposed beams and/or rafters although not always. See fig 91 Rafters are supported by roof beams at the ridge and if necessary also at intermediate points along their length. See fig 92A. The size and positioning of beams and rafters will be stated on the house plan or specification. Roof beams are supported at each end on either walls or posts. When beams or rafters are intended to be exposed, they should be wrapped in polythene for weather protection during construction.

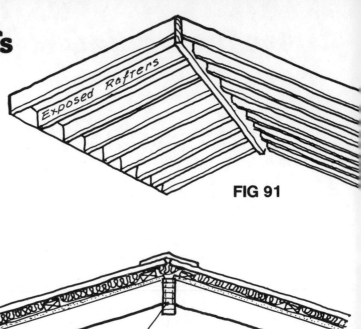

FIG 91

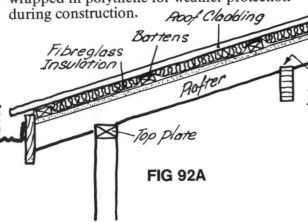

FIG 92A

FIG 92B

Rafter to Beam Connections

Ridge beams are notched to house rafter ends. See fig 93. A galvanized iron strap is taken across each pair of rafters as in fig 94. Rafters should be birdsmouthed over intermediate beam support and the specified tie down fixing applied.

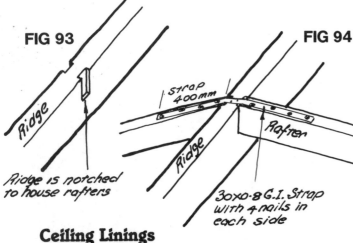

FIG 93

FIG 94

Ceiling Linings

Ceiling linings can be attached on top of the rafters prior to fixing purlins thereby exposing the rafters underneath or fixed to the underside of the rafters or battens providing a flush smooth ceiling.

When linings are attached on top of the rafters, the rafters can be spaced at 900mm centres and the centre portion of the linings are later nailed or screwed to the roof purlins or battens from underneath.

Common materials used for this purpose are T & G boards, ply with grooves to simulate boards or fibre cement sheeting.

Apply the first coat of paint or varnish to the linings prior to fixing. This will save much awkward brush cutting in work at a later date.

Cooling Cathedral Ceilings

Cathedral ceilings should contain some form of ventilation near the highest points to enable the rising hot air to escape.

It is also recommended to install fibreglass insulation directly beneath the roof cladding to reduce heat transmission. When foil is applied as a vapour barrier, it should be placed beneath the fibreglass. All vapour barrier laps should be a minimum of 150mm and be sealed with pressure sensitive vapour impervious tape. The vapour barrier should have sufficient slack between purlins to support the insulation blanket and still retain its normal thickness after attaching the roof cladding.

The fibreglass insulation is applied in blanket form from a roll and is also permitted sufficient slack between purlins to retain its normal thickness. See figure 92B. When applying fibre cement cladding or other pervious claddings, it is recommended that an additional vapour barrier be applied over the fibreglass to prevent moisture penetrating the fibreglass blanket.

Eaves Construction

A variety of designs are possible. Where level soffits are specified, A to C are commonly used. Where the overall house design necessitates the concealing of guttering, E and F methods are applied.

On Cathedral Ceiling Roofs
It is common practice to allow the soffits to remain on the rake as in E and D. On D when lining the sloping soffit, ensure the fascia board slot is clear of the bottom edge of the rafter otherwise it is difficult gaining access to the slot with the lining on the rake. When the roof pitch is very steep, access to the slot may not be possible. In this case either allow the lining to simply butt neatly up to the fascia or apply a beading over the joint. The beading will have to be shaped to fit the angle of the roof slope. Illustration E provides a good solution.

Fitting the Fascia Board
Building the eaves is simplified if slotted fascia boards are used. In order for the soffit linings to slot properly into the fascia board slot, ensure the bottom edge of the fascia is straight both ways.

How to Build Eaves
The method can vary depending on the situation or specifications or the tradesperson's preference. On brick veneer, the eaves can be framed using A,B or C methods. On A the brick walls can be built prior to eaves framing. On weatherboard construction, a batten is attached along the stud wall to support the linings as in C. Manufacturer's recommend support to be at 450mm centres. This support can either be across the eaves as in B or down the length of the eaves i.e. parallel to the walls as in C or a combination of both methods as seen in B.

The first step to framing is to level a line from the top edge of the slot in the fascia across to the stud frame at each end of the eaves length. Then spring a chalk line across the studs through the level marks. When applying method B, the wall batten is then fixed to the chalk line. The cross battens are then skew nailed to the wall batten on one side and nailed to the side of the rafters on the opposite side.

On brick veneer, noggs will be required to provide nailing for mouldings at the joint of the soffit and the brick face.

Framing Material
Cross sectional size of framing material can range from 50mm x 35mm to 70mm x 35mm depending on the spans. This is an ideal place to utilize much of the waste material lying around the job.

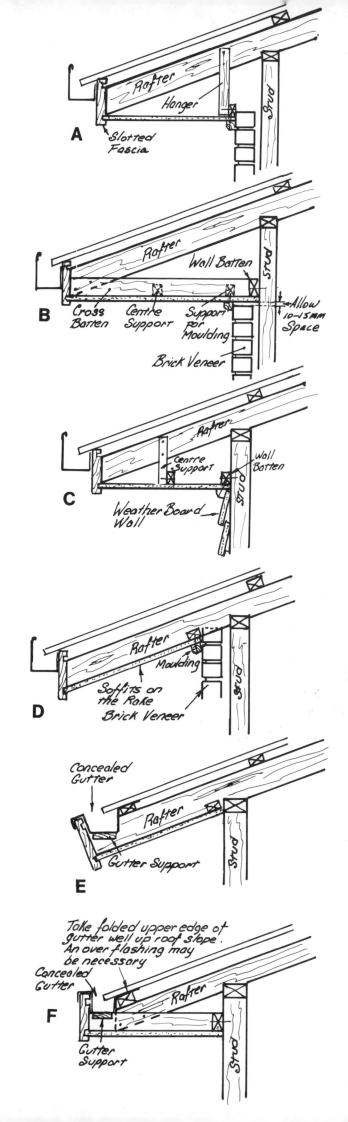

7

Rafter Lengths & Bevels

Make a Roof Plan

It is good practice to draw in pencil all the roof members on the house floor plan or make a separate roof plan similar to fig 95 1:50 scale. This will greatly assist with the calculating process and help avoid omissions. As each member is calculated it should be checked off the plan and recorded for quick reference.

How to Use the Tables

All the tables are stated in millimetres. Each table is divided up into 4 sections. The 4 shaded columns represent the Run and commence with runs of 1000's, then 100's then 10's

Example Tables

then single digits. The columns next to the Run contain the lengths of all rafters except hip and valley. The remaining column contains the lengths of hip and valley rafters.

Here is an Example
If the roof pitch is 20 degrees and the run is 2456mm:
Simply read the length beside each run column:

Run 2456:	Run mm	Rafter Length
	2000	2128
	400	426
	50	53
	6	+ 6
		Total = 2613
		rafter length

PITCH	Run (mm)	Rafter Length	Hip Length	Run (mm)	Rafter Length	Hip Length	Run (mm)	Rafter Length	Hip Length	Run (mm)	Rafter Length	Hip Length
20°	1 000	1 064	1 460	100	106	146	10	11	15	1	1	1
	2 000	2 128	2 921	200	213	292	20	21	29	2	2	3
	3 000	3 193	4 381	300	319	438	30	32	44	3	3	4
	4 000	4 257	5 841	400	426	584	40	43	58	4	4	6
	5 000	5 321	7 301	500	532	730	50	53	73	5	5	7
	6 000	6 385	8 762	600	639	876	60	64	88	6	6	9
Rise per 1000 Run = 364				700	745	1 022	70	74	102	7	7	10
				800	851	1 168	80	85	117	8	9	12
Ratio = 1:2.75				900	958	1 314	90	96	131	9	10	13

Actual Examples

The following pages 38-40 are actual examples of how to find rafter lengths using the example roof plan on page 39 and the tables. The examples cover both the major and minor roofs and are based on a pitch of 20 degrees with rafters at 600mm centres.

Major Roof Area

Ridge
The ridge length is found by deducting the building width from its length. For example using the building measurements in fig 95 on the major span.

Building length	6150mm
Building width	4950mm
Ridge length	1200mm

In gable roofs, the ridge will be the building length plus overhangs.
Ridge lengths can also be obtained by on site measurements.

The Common Rafter
In roofs of equal pitch, the run of the common rafter is exactly half the span of the roof. Where there is an unequal pitch or rise, each slope is taken separately. See unequal pitch roofs on page 6.
In the example in fig 95, the common rafter run for the major span is 2475mm. A table should be made as follows:

Common Rafter
Major Roof Run = 2475mm

Lengths from tables		
	2000 run =	2128mm
	400 run =	426mm
	70 run =	74mm
	5 run =	5mm
Common Rafter Length		2633mm

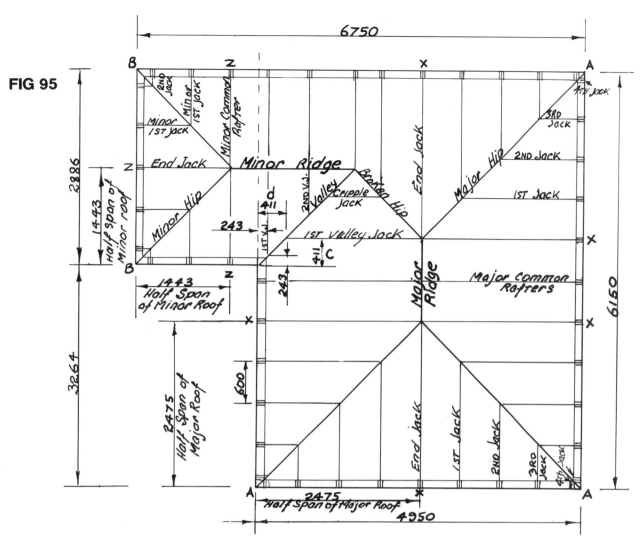

FIG 95

The Hip Rafter

(For cutting purposes the hip rafter can be measured on site or calculated as below):
Using the same example run of 2475mm, calculate the length of the hip rafter in a similar manner, reading off the lengths in the column headed 'hip rafter length'. (The run of the hip rafter is not necessary as the tables are based on the common rafter run).

Hip Rafter

Major Roof Run = 2475mm
Length from the tables:

2000 run =	2921mm
400 run =	584mm
70 run =	102mm
5 run =	7mm
	3614mm

Hip Length

The Jack Rafter (Hip & Valley Jacks)

Obtain the run of the longest jack rafter by deducting the centre to centre rafter spacing from the run of the common rafter.
The difference in length between the common rafter and the longest jack rafter is known as the 'diminish'. The diminish length is used for reducing the length of each subsequent jack rafter. The diminish can also be found by using the rafter tables. Simply call the rafter spacing measurement the run. The rafter length opposite this will be the common diminish.

In our example in fig 95 the spacing is 600mm. The rafter length for 600mm run is 639mm. Because all rafters are spaced at 600mm centres, the longest jack length will be equal to the common rafter length minus one diminish of 639mm. The second jack will be minus two diminish lengths and so on. See tables below.

When rafters are equally spaced, the difference in their lengths is called 'the common diminish'.

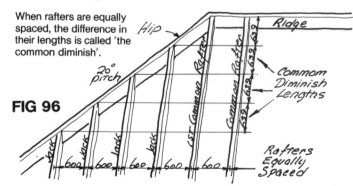

FIG 96

1st Hip Jack Rafter Length

Common Rafter Length	(C.R.) =	2633mm
Minus 1 diminish length of		639mm
1st Hip Jack Rafter Length		1994mm

2nd Hip Jack Rafter Length

C.R.	2633mm
Minus diminish of 639mm x 2	1278mm
	1355mm
2nd Hip Jack Rafter Length	

Cont

3rd Hip Jack Rafter Length

C.R.	2633mm
Minus diminish of 639mmx3	1917mm
3rd Hip Jack Rafter Length	716mm

4th Hip Jack Rafter Length

C.R.	2633mm
Minus diminish of 639mmx4	2556mm
4th Hip Jack Rafter Length	77mm

The length of the shortest jack may be increased to provide better fixing.

1st (or longest) Valley Jack

The amount by which the run of the 1st valley jack is reduced is shown on the plan. See fig 95. It can be seen that this is not a full rafter spacing but can be determined by using the dimensions known and the rafter spacings. Dimension C is calculated first. Dimension D will be the same as C. Therefore the run of the 1st valley jack will be 411mm (D) shorter than the run of the common rafter.

For Example 2475mm - 411mm = 2064mm

Length from the tables	2000 run =	2128mm
	60 run =	64mm
	4 run =	4mm
1st Valley Jack Length		2196mm

Cripple Jack Rafters

In fig 95 the run of the cripple jack is shorter than the run of the 1st valley jack by an amount equal to two rafter spacings. Its length will be the amount of the 1st valley jack less twice the diminish length.

Valley jack length	2196mm
Minus diminish 639mm x 2	1278mm
Cripple Jack Length	918mm

Broken Hip Rafter (See also page 26)

Deduct the length of the minor roof hip from the length of the major roof hip.

Major hip length	3614mm
Minor hip length	2106mm
Broken hip rafter length	1508mm

Valley Rafter

(For cutting purposes this length may be measured on site.)

The length of the valley rafter is identical to the length of the hip rafter in the minor roof

Valley length is 2106mm

Eaves Overhang Length

Calculate this as if it were a rafter. Its run will be the overhang width of 600mm.

For example:

The table overhang length for Run of

600mm	= 639mm
Hip overhang length	= 876mm

Minor Roof

Common Rafter

Minor roof run = 1443mm

Length from the tables.	1000 run =	1064mm
	400 run =	426mm
	40 run =	43mm
	3 run =	3mm
Common rafter length		1536mm

Hip Rafter

Minor roof run = 1443mm

Length from the tables.	1000 run =	1460mm
	400 run =	584mm
	40 run =	58mm
	3 run =	4mm
Hip rafter length		2106mm

1st Hip Jack Rafter

Rafter spacing 600mm = 639mm common diminish

Minor C.R. length	1536mm
Minus 1 diminish length	639mm
1st hip jack rafter length	897mm

2nd Hip Jack Rafter

Minor C.R. length	1536mm
Minus diminish of 639mmx2	1278mm
2nd hip jack rafter length	258mm

1st Valley Jack Rafter

The run of this rafter is 243mm shorter than the run of the common rafter on the minor roof. See plan.

Run of 1st valley jack 1443mm – 243mm = 1200

Length from the tables	1000 run =	1064mm
	200 run =	213mm
1st valley jack length		1277mm

2nd Valley Jack Rafter

This will be the length of the 1st valley jack minus diminish of 639mm

	1277mm
	639mm
2nd valley jack length	638mm

How to Shorten Rafters

Rafters must be reduced from their geometrical length (tables length) to their cutting length to allow for the thickness of the members to which they are attached. The cutting length of hip and valley rafters can be measured on site during erection as on pages 24 and 28. However, when these members must be precut before hand, a knowledge of how to shorten them is essential.

Common Rafter
Reduce common rafter by half the thickness of the ridge measuring square off the plumb cut bevel.

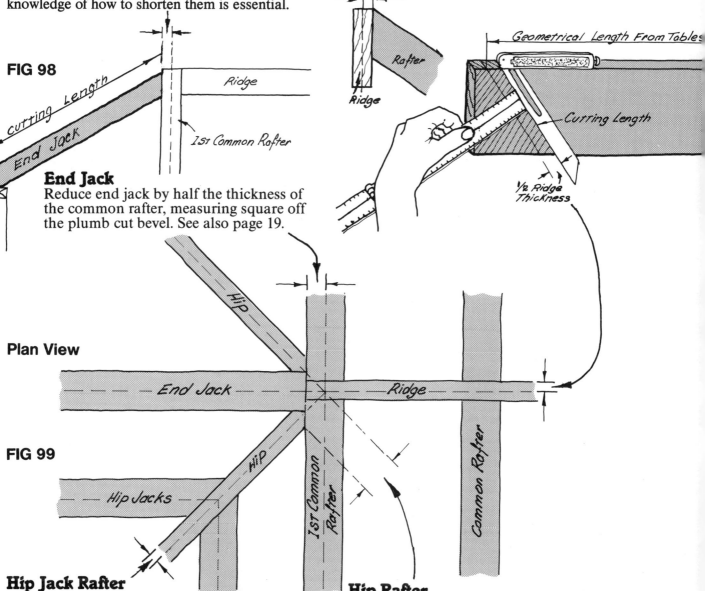

FIG 98

FIG 101

End Jack
Reduce end jack by half the thickness of the common rafter, measuring square off the plumb cut bevel. See also page 19.

Plan View

FIG 99

Hip Jack Rafter
Square the geometrical (tables) length across the top edge. Then mark the jack edge cut bevel through the centre of the squared line. Reduce this length by half the thickness of the hip rafter measuring square off the edge bevel line.

Hip Rafter
Mark out the birdsmouth then measure the geometrical (tables) length on to the face of the hip and mark the top end plumb bevel as in figs 46 and 47, page 25. To obtain the shortened length, draw a full size plan view of the hip top end connection and measure the plan length of the deduction as shown above. Make this deduction on the hip measuring square off the face bevel plumb lines.

FIG 100

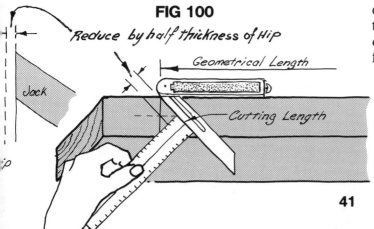

41

Cont.

Valley Rafter (see pages 28 for the on site measuring method)

Step 1 Measure and mark the geometrical length on the side of the valley and square a line across the top edge. The geometrical length of the valley rafter is identical to that for the hip rafter in the minor roof.

Step 2 Mark the hip edge bevel through the intersection of the squared line and the edge centre line. See fig 103

Step 3 The top end of valleys have two end cuts. Therefore, two shortenings are required. The bevel cut aligning with the minor ridge is the hip edge bevel and is reduced by half the thickness of the minor ridge measuring square off the hip edge bevel. The bevel aligning with the broken hip is just squared across the edge and then reduced by half the thickness of the broken hip measuring at 90 degrees off the squared line. See fig 103

FIG 103

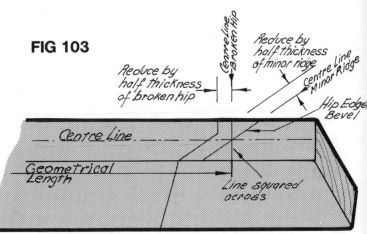

Valley Jack Rafters

The shortening of the upper end is the same as for the common rafter. The lower end is applied the same as for hip jacks except that the reduction is half the thickness of the valley rafter.

Cripple Jack Rafters

The shortening of the upper and lower end is the same as for hip jacks except that the lower end is reduced by half the thickness of the valley rafter.

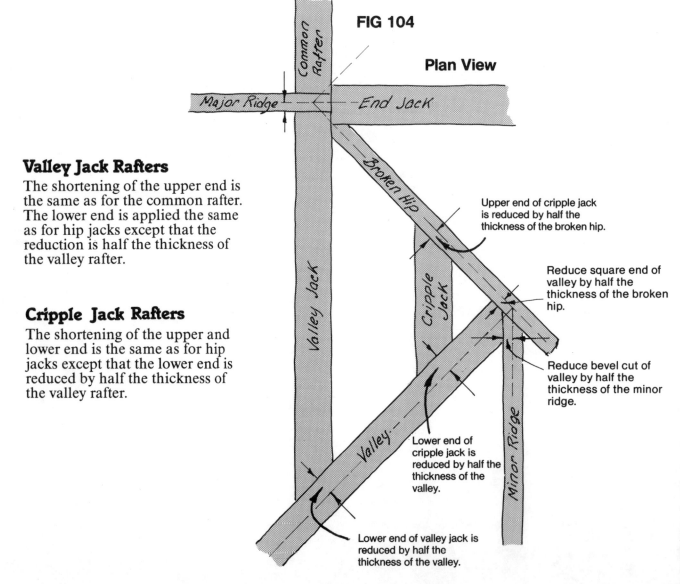

FIG 104

Plan View

Tables & Bevels

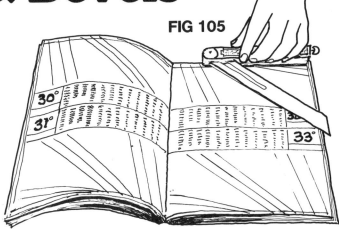

FIG 105

How to Use the Bevels

In the following pages, the bevel angles required in a hip and valley roof have been drawn above and below their accompanying table. To use them, simply adjust the bevel tool to the appropriate angle, holding the stock of the bevel on the base line. See fig 105 and sighting directly from above. Do not hold the stock on the edge of the page. After tightening the thumb screw, apply the bevel again to the angle to check for accuracy.

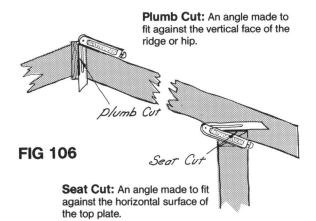

Plumb Cut: An angle made to fit against the vertical face of the ridge or hip.

Plumb Cut

FIG 106

Seat Cut

Seat Cut: An angle made to fit against the horizontal surface of the top plate.

Edge Cut: An angle cut on the narrow surface or edge of a roof member.

Edge Cut

FIG 107

Face Cut

Face Cut: An angle cut in the widest surface or face of a roof member.

Run (mm)	Rafter Length	Hip Length	Run (mm)	Rafter Length	Hip Length	Run (mm)	Rafter Length	Hip Length	Run (mm)	Rafter Length	Hip Length	PITCH
1 000	1 004	1 417	100	100	142	10	10	14	1	1	1	
2 000	2 008	2 834	200	201	283	20	20	28	2	2	3	
3 000	3 011	4 251	300	301	425	30	30	43	3	3	4	**5°**
4 000	4 015	5 668	400	402	567	40	40	57	4	4	6	
5 000	5 019	7 085	500	502	708	50	50	71	5	5	7	
6 000	6 023	8 502	600	602	850	60	60	85	6	6	9	
			700	703	992	70	70	99	7	7	10	Rise per 1000 Run
			800	803	1 134	80	80	113	8	8	11	= 88
			900	903	1 275	90	90	128	9	9	13	Ratio = 1:11.43

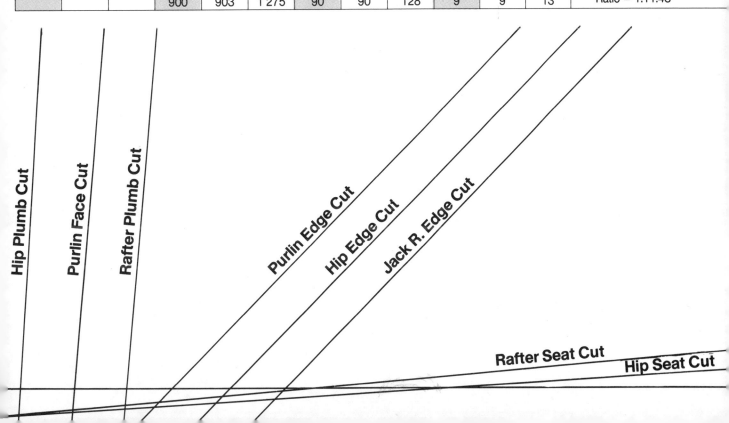

Hip Plumb Cut

Purlin Face Cut

Rafter Plumb Cut

Purlin Edge Cut

Hip Edge Cut

Jack R. Edge Cut

Rafter Seat Cut

Hip Seat Cut

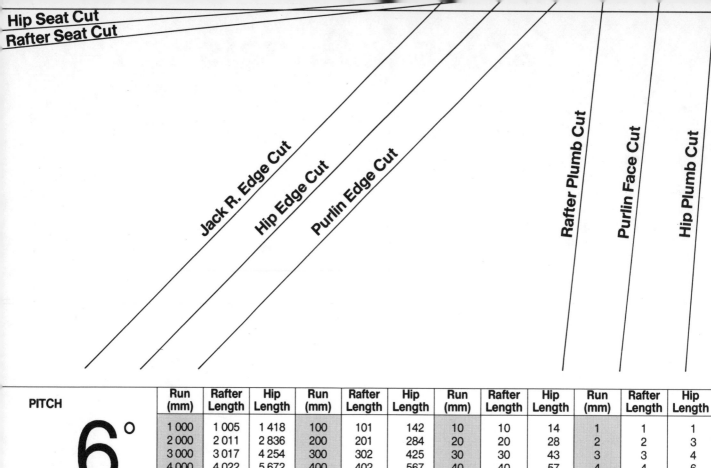

Hip Seat Cut
Rafter Seat Cut

Jack R. Edge Cut · Hip Edge Cut · Purlin Edge Cut · Rafter Plumb Cut · Purlin Face Cut · Hip Plumb Cut

PITCH 6°

Rise per 1000 Run = 105
Ratio = 1:9.51

Run (mm)	Rafter Length	Hip Length	Run (mm)	Rafter Length	Hip Length	Run (mm)	Rafter Length	Hip Length	Run (mm)	Rafter Length	Hip Length
1 000	1 005	1 418	100	101	142	10	10	14	1	1	1
2 000	2 011	2 836	200	201	284	20	20	28	2	2	3
3 000	3 017	4 254	300	302	425	30	30	43	3	3	4
4 000	4 022	5 672	400	402	567	40	40	57	4	4	6
5 000	5 028	7 091	500	503	709	50	50	71	5	5	7
6 000	6 033	8 509	600	603	851	60	60	85	6	6	9
			700	704	993	70	70	99	7	7	10
			800	804	1 134	80	80	113	8	8	11
			900	905	1 276	90	90	128	9	9	13

PITCH 7°

Rise per 1000 Run = 123
Ratio = 1:8.14

Run (mm)	Rafter Length	Hip Length	Run (mm)	Rafter Length	Hip Length	Run (mm)	Rafter Length	Hip Length	Run (mm)	Rafter Length	Hip Length
1 000	1 008	1 420	100	101	142	10	10	14	1	1	1
2 000	2 015	2 839	200	202	284	20	20	28	2	2	3
3 000	3 023	4 259	300	302	426	30	30	43	3	3	4
4 000	4 030	5 678	400	403	568	40	40	57	4	4	6
5 000	5 038	7 098	500	504	710	50	50	71	5	5	7
6 000	6 045	8 517	600	605	852	60	60	85	6	6	9
			700	705	994	70	71	99	7	7	10
			800	806	1 136	80	81	114	8	8	11
			900	907	1 278	90	91	128	9	9	13

Hip Plumb Cut · Purlin Face Cut · Rafter Plumb Cut · Purlin Edge Cut · Hip Edge Cut · Jack R. Edge Cut

Rafter Seat Cut · **Hip Seat Cut**

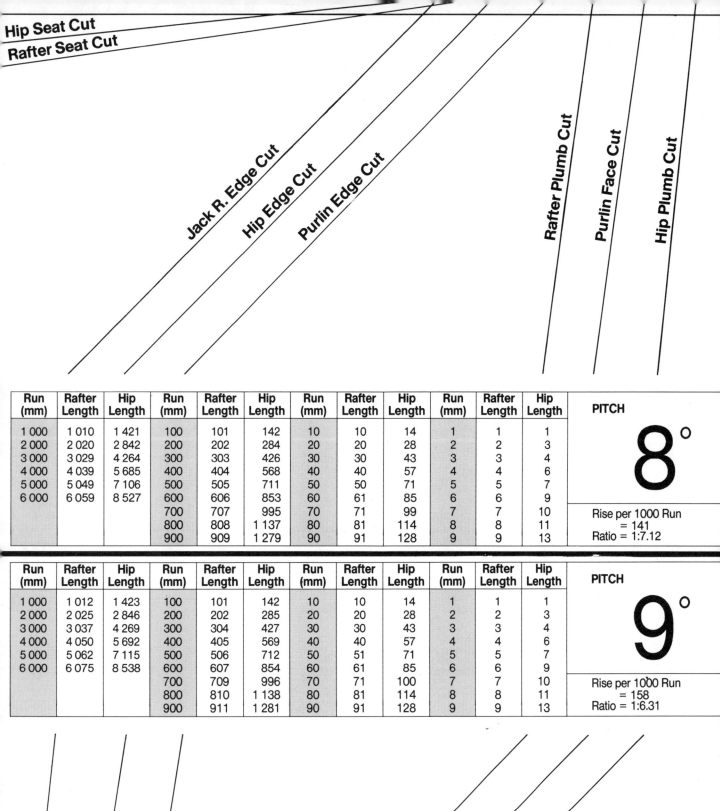

Hip Seat Cut
Rafter Seat Cut

Jack R. Edge Cut · Hip Edge Cut · Purlin Edge Cut · Rafter Plumb Cut · Purlin Face Cut · Hip Plumb Cut

Run (mm)	Rafter Length	Hip Length	Run (mm)	Rafter Length	Hip Length	Run (mm)	Rafter Length	Hip Length	Run (mm)	Rafter Length	Hip Length	PITCH
1 000	1 010	1 421	100	101	142	10	10	14	1	1	1	**8°**
2 000	2 020	2 842	200	202	284	20	20	28	2	2	3	
3 000	3 029	4 264	300	303	426	30	30	43	3	3	4	
4 000	4 039	5 685	400	404	568	40	40	57	4	4	6	
5 000	5 049	7 106	500	505	711	50	50	71	5	5	7	
6 000	6 059	8 527	600	606	853	60	61	85	6	6	9	Rise per 1000 Run = 141
			700	707	995	70	71	99	7	7	10	Ratio = 1:7.12
			800	808	1 137	80	81	114	8	8	11	
			900	909	1 279	90	91	128	9	9	13	

Run (mm)	Rafter Length	Hip Length	Run (mm)	Rafter Length	Hip Length	Run (mm)	Rafter Length	Hip Length	Run (mm)	Rafter Length	Hip Length	PITCH
1 000	1 012	1 423	100	101	142	10	10	14	1	1	1	**9°**
2 000	2 025	2 846	200	202	285	20	20	28	2	2	3	
3 000	3 037	4 269	300	304	427	30	30	43	3	3	4	
4 000	4 050	5 692	400	405	569	40	40	57	4	4	6	
5 000	5 062	7 115	500	506	712	50	51	71	5	5	7	
6 000	6 075	8 538	600	607	854	60	61	85	6	6	9	Rise per 1000 Run = 158
			700	709	996	70	71	100	7	7	10	Ratio = 1:6.31
			800	810	1 138	80	81	114	8	8	11	
			900	911	1 281	90	91	128	9	9	13	

Hip Plumb Cut · Purlin Face Cut · Rafter Plumb Cut · Purlin Edge Cut · Hip Edge Cut · Jack R. Edge Cut

Rafter Seat Cut
Hip Seat Cut

Hip Seat Cut

Rafter Seat Cut

Jack R. Edge Cut

Hip Edge Cut

Purlin Edge Cut

Rafter Plumb Cut

Purlin Face Cut

Hip Plumb Cut

PITCH **10°**	Run (mm)	Rafter Length	Hip Length	Run (mm)	Rafter Length	Hip Length	Run (mm)	Rafter Length	Hip Length	Run (mm)	Rafter Length	Hip Length
	1 000	1 015	1 425	100	102	143	10	10	14	1	1	1
	2 000	2 031	2 850	200	203	285	20	20	29	2	2	3
	3 000	3 046	4 275	300	305	428	30	30	43	3	3	4
	4 000	4 062	5 701	400	406	570	40	41	57	4	4	6
	5 000	5 077	7 126	500	508	713	50	51	71	5	5	7
Rise per 1000 Run = 176 Ratio = 1:5.67	6 000	6 093	8 551	600	609	855	60	61	86	6	6	9
				700	711	998	70	71	100	7	7	10
				800	812	1 140	80	81	114	8	8	11
				900	914	1 283	90	91	128	9	9	13

PITCH **11°**	Run (mm)	Rafter Length	Hip Length	Run (mm)	Rafter Length	Hip Length	Run (mm)	Rafter Length	Hip Length	Run (mm)	Rafter Length	Hip Length
	1 000	1 019	1 428	100	102	143	10	10	14	1	1	1
	2 000	2 037	2 855	200	204	286	20	20	29	2	2	3
	3 000	3 056	4 283	300	306	428	30	31	43	3	3	4
	4 000	4 075	5 710	400	407	571	40	41	57	4	4	6
	5 000	5 094	7 138	500	509	714	50	51	71	5	5	7
Rise per 1000 Run = 194 Ratio = 1:5.14	6 000	6 112	8 565	600	611	857	60	61	86	6	6	9
				700	713	999	70	71	100	7	7	10
				800	815	1 142	80	81	114	8	8	11
				900	917	1 285	90	92	128	9	9	13

Hip Plumb Cut

Purlin Face Cut

Rafter Plumb Cut

Purlin Edge Cut

Hip Edge Cut

Jack R. Edge Cut

Rafter Seat Cut

Hip Seat Cut

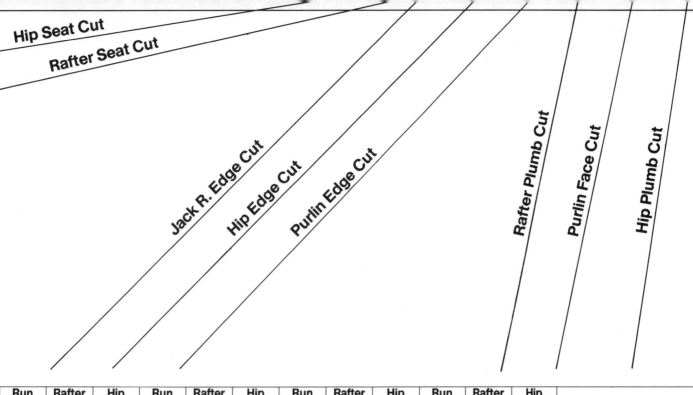

Run (mm)	Rafter Length	Hip Length	Run (mm)	Rafter Length	Hip Length	Run (mm)	Rafter Length	Hip Length	Run (mm)	Rafter Length	Hip Length	PITCH
1 000	1 022	1 430	100	102	143	10	10	14	1	1	1	**12°**
2 000	2 045	2 860	200	204	286	20	20	29	2	2	3	
3 000	3 067	4 290	300	307	429	30	31	43	3	3	4	
4 000	4 089	5 720	400	409	572	40	41	57	4	4	6	
5 000	5 112	7 150	500	511	715	50	51	72	5	5	7	
6 000	6 134	8 581	600	613	858	60	61	86	6	6	9	
			700	716	1 001	70	72	100	7	7	10	Rise per 1000 Run
			800	818	1 144	80	82	114	8	8	11	= 213
			900	920	1 287	90	92	129	9	9	13	Ratio = 1:4.7

Run (mm)	Rafter Length	Hip Length	Run (mm)	Rafter Length	Hip Length	Run (mm)	Rafter Length	Hip Length	Run (mm)	Rafter Length	Hip Length	PITCH
1 000	1 026	1 433	100	103	143	10	10	14	1	1	1	**13°**
2 000	2 053	2 866	200	205	287	20	21	29	2	2	3	
3 000	3 079	4 299	300	308	430	30	31	43	3	3	4	
4 000	4 105	5 732	400	411	573	40	41	57	4	4	6	
5 000	5 132	7 165	500	513	716	50	51	72	5	5	7	
6 000	6 158	8 598	600	616	860	60	62	86	6	6	9	
			700	718	1 003	70	72	100	7	7	10	Rise per 1000 Run
			800	821	1 146	80	82	115	8	8	11	= 231
			900	924	1 290	90	92	129	9	9	13	Ratio = 1:4.33

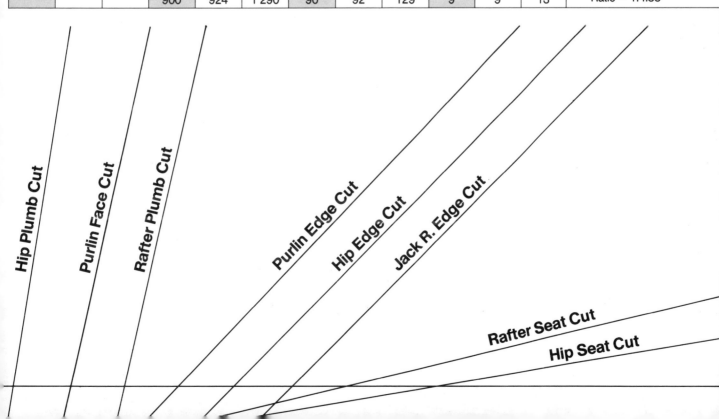

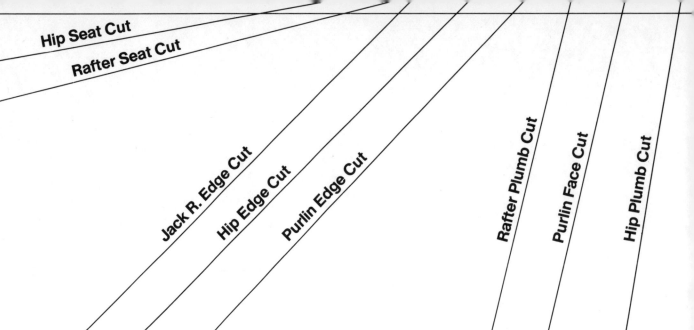

Hip Seat Cut · Rafter Seat Cut · Jack R. Edge Cut · Hip Edge Cut · Purlin Edge Cut · Rafter Plumb Cut · Purlin Face Cut · Hip Plumb Cut

PITCH 14°

Run (mm)	Rafter Length	Hip Length	Run (mm)	Rafter Length	Hip Length	Run (mm)	Rafter Length	Hip Length	Run (mm)	Rafter Length	Hip Length
1 000	1 031	1 436	100	103	144	10	10	14	1	1	1
2 000	2 061	2 872	200	206	287	20	21	29	2	2	3
3 000	3 092	4 308	300	309	431	30	31	43	3	3	4
4 000	4 122	5 744	400	412	574	40	41	57	4	4	6
5 000	5 153	7 180	500	515	718	50	52	72	5	5	7
6 000	6 184	8 616	600	618	862	60	62	86	6	6	9
			700	721	1 005	70	72	101	7	7	10
			800	824	1 149	80	82	115	8	8	11
			900	928	1 292	90	93	129	9	9	13

Rise per 1000 Run = 249
Ratio = 1:4.01

PITCH 15°

Run (mm)	Rafter Length	Hip Length	Run (mm)	Rafter Length	Hip Length	Run (mm)	Rafter Length	Hip Length	Run (mm)	Rafter Length	Hip Length
1 000	1 035	1 439	100	104	144	10	10	14	1	1	1
2 000	2 071	2 879	200	207	288	20	21	29	2	2	3
3 000	3 106	4 318	300	311	432	30	31	43	3	3	4
4 000	4 141	5 757	400	414	576	40	41	58	4	4	6
5 000	5 176	7 197	500	518	720	50	52	72	5	5	7
6 000	6 212	8 636	600	621	864	60	62	86	6	6	9
			700	725	1 008	70	72	101	7	7	10
			800	828	1 151	80	83	115	8	8	12
			900	932	1 295	90	93	130	9	9	13

Rise per 1000 Run = 268
Ratio = 1:3.73

Hip Plumb Cut · Purlin Face Cut · Rafter Plumb Cut · Purlin Edge Cut · Hip Edge Cut · Jack R. Edge Cut · Rafter Seat Cut · Hip Seat Cut

Hip Seat Cut

Rafter Seat Cut

Jack R. Edge Cut

Hip Edge Cut

Purlin Edge Cut

Rafter Plumb Cut

Purlin Face Cut

Hip Plumb Cut

Run (mm)	Rafter Length	Hip Length	Run (mm)	Rafter Length	Hip Length	Run (mm)	Rafter Length	Hip Length	Run (mm)	Rafter Length	Hip Length	PITCH
1 000	1 040	1 443	100	104	144	10	10	14	1	1	1	**16°**
2 000	2 081	2 886	200	208	289	20	21	29	2	2	3	
3 000	3 121	4 329	300	312	433	30	31	43	3	3	4	
4 000	4 161	5 772	400	416	577	40	42	58	4	4	6	
5 000	5 201	7 215	500	520	721	50	52	72	5	5	7	
6 000	6 242	8 658	600	624	866	60	62	87	6	6	9	Rise per 1000 Run
			700	728	1 010	70	73	101	7	7	10	= 287
			800	832	1 154	80	83	115	8	8	12	Ratio = 1:3.49
			900	936	1 299	90	94	130	9	9	13	

Run (mm)	Rafter Length	Hip Length	Run (mm)	Rafter Length	Hip Length	Run (mm)	Rafter Length	Hip Length	Run (mm)	Rafter Length	Hip Length	PITCH
1 000	1 046	1 447	100	105	145	10	10	14	1	1	1	**17°**
2 000	2 091	2 894	200	209	289	20	21	29	2	2	3	
3 000	3 137	4 341	300	314	434	30	31	43	3	3	4	
4 000	4 183	5 788	400	418	579	40	42	58	4	4	6	
5 000	5 228	7 234	500	523	723	50	52	72	5	5	7	
6 000	6 274	8 681	600	627	868	60	63	87	6	6	9	Rise per 1000 Run
			700	732	1 013	70	73	101	7	7	10	= 306
			800	837	1 158	80	84	116	8	8	12	Ratio = 1:3.27
			900	941	1 302	90	94	130	9	9	13	

Hip Plumb Cut

Purlin Face Cut

Rafter Plumb Cut

Purlin Edge Cut

Hip Edge Cut

Jack R. Edge Cut

Rafter Seat Cut

Hip Seat Cut

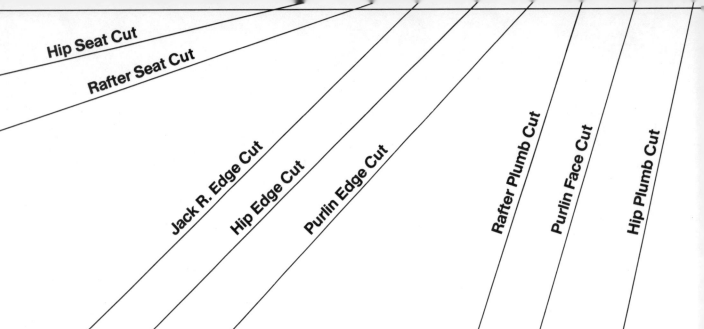

Hip Seat Cut
Rafter Seat Cut
Jack R. Edge Cut
Hip Edge Cut
Purlin Edge Cut
Rafter Plumb Cut
Purlin Face Cut
Hip Plumb Cut

PITCH	Run (mm)	Rafter Length	Hip Length	Run (mm)	Rafter Length	Hip Length	Run (mm)	Rafter Length	Hip Length	Run (mm)	Rafter Length	Hip Length
18°	1 000	1 051	1 451	100	105	145	10	11	15	1	1	1
	2 000	2 103	2 902	200	210	290	20	21	29	2	2	3
	3 000	3 154	4 353	300	315	435	30	32	44	3	3	4
	4 000	4 206	5 804	400	421	580	40	42	58	4	4	6
	5 000	5 257	7 255	500	526	726	50	53	73	5	5	7
	6 000	6 309	8 706	600	631	871	60	63	87	6	6	9
Rise per 1000 Run = 325				700	736	1 016	70	74	102	7	7	10
Ratio = 1:3.08				800	841	1 161	80	84	116	8	8	12
				900	946	1 306	90	95	131	9	9	13

PITCH	Run (mm)	Rafter Length	Hip Length	Run (mm)	Rafter Length	Hip Length	Run (mm)	Rafter Length	Hip Length	Run (mm)	Rafter Length	Hip Length
19°	1 000	1 058	1 456	100	106	146	10	11	15	1	1	1
	2 000	2 115	2 911	200	212	291	20	21	29	2	2	3
	3 000	3 173	4 367	300	317	437	30	32	44	3	3	4
	4 000	4 230	5 822	400	423	582	40	42	58	4	4	6
	5 000	5 288	7 278	500	529	728	50	53	73	5	5	7
	6 000	6 346	8 733	600	635	873	60	63	87	6	6	9
Rise per 1000 Run = 344				700	740	1 019	70	74	102	7	7	10
Ratio = 1:2.9				800	846	1 164	80	85	116	8	8	12
				900	952	1 310	90	95	131	9	10	13

Hip Plumb Cut
Purlin Face Cut
Rafter Plumb Cut
Purlin Edge Cut
Hip Edge Cut
Jack R. Edge Cut
Rafter Seat Cut
Hip Seat Cut

Hip Seat Cut

Rafter Seat Cut

Jack R. Edge Cut

Hip Edge Cut

Purlin Edge Cut

Rafter Plumb Cut

Purlin Face Cut

Hip Plumb Cut

Run (mm)	Rafter Length	Hip Length	Run (mm)	Rafter Length	Hip Length	Run (mm)	Rafter Length	Hip Length	Run (mm)	Rafter Length	Hip Length	PITCH
1 000	1 064	1 460	100	106	146	10	11	15	1	1	1	**20°**
2 000	2 128	2 921	200	213	292	20	21	29	2	2	3	
3 000	3 193	4 381	300	319	438	30	32	44	3	3	4	
4 000	4 257	5 841	400	426	584	40	43	58	4	4	6	
5 000	5 321	7 301	500	532	730	50	53	73	5	5	7	
6 000	6 385	8 762	600	639	876	60	64	88	6	6	9	
			700	745	1 022	70	74	102	7	7	10	Rise per 1000 Run = 364
			800	851	1 168	80	85	117	8	9	12	Ratio = 1:2.75
			900	958	1 314	90	96	131	9	10	13	

Run (mm)	Rafter Length	Hip Length	Run (mm)	Rafter Length	Hip Length	Run (mm)	Rafter Length	Hip Length	Run (mm)	Rafter Length	Hip Length	PITCH
1 000	1 071	1 465	100	107	147	10	11	15	1	1	1	**21°**
2 000	2 142	2 931	200	214	293	20	21	29	2	2	3	
3 000	3 213	4 396	300	321	440	30	32	44	3	3	4	
4 000	4 285	5 862	400	428	586	40	43	59	4	4	6	
5 000	5 356	7 327	500	536	733	50	54	73	5	5	7	
6 000	6 427	8 792	600	643	879	60	64	88	6	6	9	
			700	750	1 026	70	75	103	7	7	10	Rise per 1000 Run = 384
			800	857	1 172	80	86	117	8	9	12	Ratio = 1:2.61
			900	964	1 319	90	96	132	9	10	13	

Hip Plumb Cut

Purlin Face Cut

Rafter Plumb Cut

Purlin Edge Cut

Hip Edge Cut

Jack R. Edge Cut

Rafter Seat Cut

Hip Seat Cut

Hip Seat Cut
Rafter Seat Cut
Jack R. Edge Cut
Hip Edge Cut
Purlin Edge Cut
Rafter Plumb Cut
Purlin Face Cut
Hip Plumb Cut

PITCH 22°

Rise per 1000 Run = 404
Ratio = 1:2.48

Run (mm)	Rafter Length	Hip Length	Run (mm)	Rafter Length	Hip Length	Run (mm)	Rafter Length	Hip Length	Run (mm)	Rafter Length	Hip Length
1 000	1 079	1 471	100	108	147	10	11	15	1	1	1
2 000	2 157	2 942	200	216	294	20	22	29	2	2	3
3 000	3 236	4 412	300	324	441	30	32	44	3	3	4
4 000	4 314	5 883	400	431	588	40	43	59	4	4	6
5 000	5 393	7 354	500	539	735	50	54	74	5	5	7
6 000	6 471	8 825	600	647	882	60	65	88	6	6	9
			700	755	1 030	70	75	103	7	8	10
			800	863	1 177	80	86	118	8	9	12
			900	971	1 324	90	97	132	9	10	13

PITCH 23°

Rise per 1000 Run = 424
Ratio = 1:2.36

Run (mm)	Rafter Length	Hip Length	Run (mm)	Rafter Length	Hip Length	Run (mm)	Rafter Length	Hip Length	Run (mm)	Rafter Length	Hip Length
1 000	1 086	1 477	100	109	148	10	11	15	1	1	1
2 000	2 173	2 953	200	217	295	20	22	30	2	2	3
3 000	3 259	4 430	300	326	443	30	33	44	3	3	4
4 000	4 345	5 906	400	435	591	40	43	59	4	4	6
5 000	5 432	7 383	500	543	738	50	54	74	5	5	7
6 000	6 518	8 859	600	652	886	60	65	89	6	7	9
			700	760	1 034	70	76	103	7	8	10
			800	869	1 181	80	87	118	8	9	12
			900	978	1 329	90	98	133	9	10	13

Hip Plumb Cut
Purlin Face Cut
Rafter Plumb Cut
Purlin Edge Cut
Hip Edge Cut
Jack R. Edge Cut
Rafter Seat Cut
Hip Seat Cut

Hip Seat Cut

Rafter Seat Cut

Jack R. Edge Cut

Hip Edge Cut

Purlin Edge Cut

Rafter Plumb Cut

Purlin Face Cut

Hip Plumb Cut

Run (mm)	Rafter Length	Hip Length	Run (mm)	Rafter Length	Hip Length	Run (mm)	Rafter Length	Hip Length	Run (mm)	Rafter Length	Hip Length	PITCH
1 000	1 095	1 483	100	109	148	10	11	15	1	1	1	
2 000	2 189	2 965	200	219	297	20	22	30	2	2	3	
3 000	3 284	4 448	300	328	445	30	33	44	3	3	4	**24°**
4 000	4 379	5 931	400	438	593	40	44	59	4	4	6	
5 000	5 473	7 413	500	547	741	50	55	74	5	5	7	
6 000	6 568	8 896	600	657	890	60	66	89	6	7	9	
			700	766	1 038	70	77	104	7	8	10	Rise per 1000 Run = 445
			800	876	1 186	80	88	119	8	9	12	Ratio = 1:2.25
			900	985	1 334	90	99	133	9	10	13	

Run (mm)	Rafter Length	Hip Length	Run (mm)	Rafter Length	Hip Length	Run (mm)	Rafter Length	Hip Length	Run (mm)	Rafter Length	Hip Length	PITCH
1 000	1 103	1 489	100	110	149	10	11	15	1	1	1	
2 000	2 207	2 978	200	221	298	20	22	30	2	2	3	
3 000	3 310	4 467	300	331	447	30	33	45	3	3	4	**25°**
4 000	4 414	5 956	400	441	596	40	44	60	4	4	6	
5 000	5 517	7 446	500	552	745	50	55	74	5	6	7	
6 000	6 620	8 935	600	662	893	60	66	89	6	7	9	
			700	772	1 042	70	77	104	7	8	10	Rise per 1000 Run = 466
			800	883	1 191	80	88	119	8	9	12	Ratio = 1:2.14
			900	993	1 340	90	99	134	9	10	13	

Hip Plumb Cut

Purlin Face Cut

Rafter Plumb Cut

Purlin Edge Cut

Hip Edge Cut

Jack R. Edge Cut

Rafter Seat Cut

Hip Seat Cut

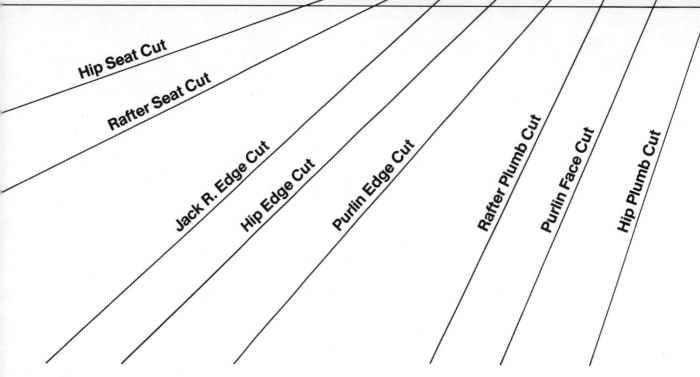

PITCH 26°	Run (mm)	Rafter Length	Hip Length	Run (mm)	Rafter Length	Hip Length	Run (mm)	Rafter Length	Hip Length	Run (mm)	Rafter Length	Hip Length
	1 000	1 113	1 496	100	111	150	10	11	15	1	1	1
	2 000	2 225	2 992	200	223	299	20	22	30	2	2	3
	3 000	3 338	4 488	300	334	449	30	33	45	3	3	4
	4 000	4 450	5 984	400	445	598	40	45	60	4	4	6
	5 000	5 563	7 480	500	556	748	50	56	75	5	6	7
	6 000	6 676	8 976	600	668	898	60	67	90	6	7	9
Rise per 1000 Run = 488				700	779	1 047	70	78	105	7	8	10
Ratio = 1:2.05				800	890	1 197	80	89	120	8	9	12
				900	1 001	1 346	90	100	135	9	10	13

PITCH 27°	Run (mm)	Rafter Length	Hip Length	Run (mm)	Rafter Length	Hip Length	Run (mm)	Rafter Length	Hip Length	Run (mm)	Rafter Length	Hip Length
	1 000	1 122	1 503	100	112	150	10	11	15	1	1	2
	2 000	2 245	3 006	200	224	301	20	22	30	2	2	3
	3 000	3 367	4 510	300	337	451	30	34	45	3	3	5
	4 000	4 489	6 013	400	449	601	40	45	60	4	4	6
	5 000	5 612	7 516	500	561	752	50	56	75	5	6	8
	6 000	6 734	9 019	600	673	902	60	67	90	6	7	9
Rise per 1000 Run = 510				700	786	1 052	70	79	105	7	8	11
Ratio = 1:1.96				800	898	1 203	80	90	120	8	9	12
				900	1 010	1 353	90	101	135	9	10	14

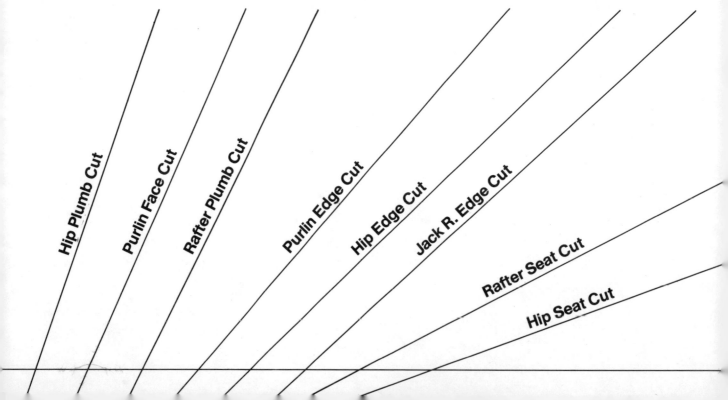

Hip Seat Cut

Rafter Seat Cut

Jack R. Edge Cut

Hip Edge Cut

Purlin Edge Cut

Rafter Plumb Cut

Purlin Face Cut

Hip Plumb Cut

Run (mm)	Rafter Length	Hip Length	Run (mm)	Rafter Length	Hip Length	Run (mm)	Rafter Length	Hip Length	Run (mm)	Rafter Length	Hip Length	PITCH
1 000	1 133	1 511	100	113	151	10	11	15	1	1	2	**28°**
2 000	2 265	3 022	200	227	302	20	23	30	2	2	3	
3 000	3 398	4 533	300	340	453	30	34	45	3	3	5	
4 000	4 530	6 043	400	453	604	40	45	60	4	5	6	
5 000	5 663	7 554	500	566	755	50	57	76	5	6	8	
6 000	6 795	9 065	600	680	907	60	68	91	6	7	9	
			700	793	1 058	70	79	106	7	8	11	Rise per 1000 Run
			800	906	1 209	80	91	121	8	9	12	= 532
			900	1 019	1 360	90	102	136	9	10	14	Ratio = 1:1.88

Run (mm)	Rafter Length	Hip Length	Run (mm)	Rafter Length	Hip Length	Run (mm)	Rafter Length	Hip Length	Run (mm)	Rafter Length	Hip Length	PITCH
1 000	1 143	1 519	100	114	152	10	11	15	1	1	2	**29°**
2 000	2 287	3 038	200	229	304	20	23	30	2	2	3	
3 000	3 430	4 557	300	343	456	30	34	46	3	3	5	
4 000	4 573	6 076	400	457	608	40	46	61	4	5	6	
5 000	5 717	7 595	500	572	759	50	57	76	5	6	8	
6 000	6 860	9 114	600	686	911	60	69	91	6	7	9	
			700	800	1 063	70	80	106	7	8	11	Rise per 1000 Run
			800	915	1 215	80	91	122	8	9	12	= 554
			900	1 029	1 367	90	103	137	9	10	14	Ratio = 1:1.8

Hip Plumb Cut

Purlin Face Cut

Rafter Plumb Cut

Purlin Edge Cut

Hip Edge Cut

Jack R. Edge Cut

Rafter Seat Cut

Hip Seat Cut

Hip Seat Cut

Rafter Seat Cut

Jack R. Edge Cut

Hip Edge Cut

Purlin Edge Cut

Rafter Plumb Cut

Purlin Face Cut

Hip Plumb Cut

PITCH 30°

Rise per 1000 Run = 577
Ratio = 1:1.73

Run (mm)	Rafter Length	Hip Length	Run (mm)	Rafter Length	Hip Length	Run (mm)	Rafter Length	Hip Length	Run (mm)	Rafter Length	Hip Length
1 000	1 155	1 528	100	115	153	10	12	15	1	1	2
2 000	2 309	3 055	200	231	306	20	23	31	2	2	3
3 000	3 464	4 583	300	346	458	30	35	46	3	3	5
4 000	4 619	6 110	400	462	611	40	46	61	4	5	6
5 000	5 774	7 638	500	577	764	50	58	76	5	6	8
6 000	6 928	9 165	600	693	917	60	69	92	6	7	9
			700	808	1 069	70	81	107	7	8	11
			800	924	1 222	80	92	122	8	9	12
			900	1 039	1 375	90	104	137	9	10	14

PITCH 31°

Rise per 1000 Run = 601
Ratio = 1:1.66

Run (mm)	Rafter Length	Hip Length	Run (mm)	Rafter Length	Hip Length	Run (mm)	Rafter Length	Hip Length	Run (mm)	Rafter Length	Hip Length
1 000	1 167	1 537	100	117	154	10	12	15	1	1	2
2 000	2 333	3 073	200	233	307	20	23	31	2	2	3
3 000	3 500	4 610	300	350	461	30	35	46	3	3	5
4 000	4 667	6 146	400	467	615	40	47	61	4	5	6
5 000	5 833	7 683	500	583	768	50	58	77	5	6	8
6 000	7 000	9 219	600	700	922	60	70	92	6	7	9
			700	817	1 076	70	82	108	7	8	11
			800	933	1 229	80	93	123	8	9	12
			900	1 050	1 383	90	105	138	9	10	14

Hip Plumb Cut

Purlin Face Cut

Rafter Plumb Cut

Purlin Edge Cut

Hip Edge Cut

Jack R. Edge Cut

Rafter Seat Cut

Hip Seat Cut

Hip Seat Cut
Rafter Seat Cut
Jack R. Edge Cut
Hip Edge Cut
Purlin Edge Cut
Rafter Plumb Cut
Purlin Face Cut
Hip Plumb Cut

Run (mm)	Rafter Length	Hip Length	Run (mm)	Rafter Length	Hip Length	Run (mm)	Rafter Length	Hip Length	Run (mm)	Rafter Length	Hip Length	PITCH
1 000	1 179	1 546	100	118	155	10	12	15	1	1	2	**32°**
2 000	2 358	3 092	200	236	309	20	24	31	2	2	3	
3 000	3 538	4 638	300	354	464	30	35	46	3	4	5	
4 000	4 717	6 184	400	472	618	40	47	62	4	5	6	
5 000	5 896	7 731	500	590	773	50	59	77	5	6	8	
6 000	7 075	9 277	600	708	928	60	71	93	6	7	9	
			700	825	1 082	70	83	108	7	8	11	Rise per 1000 Run = 625
			800	943	1 237	80	94	124	8	9	12	Ratio = 1:1.6
			900	1 061	1 392	90	106	139	9	11	14	

Run (mm)	Rafter Length	Hip Length	Run (mm)	Rafter Length	Hip Length	Run (mm)	Rafter Length	Hip Length	Run (mm)	Rafter Length	Hip Length	PITCH
1 000	1 192	1 556	100	119	156	10	12	16	1	1	2	**33°**
2 000	2 385	3 112	200	238	311	20	24	31	2	2	3	
3 000	3 577	4 669	300	358	467	30	36	47	3	4	5	
4 000	4 769	6 225	400	477	622	40	48	62	4	5	6	
5 000	5 962	7 781	500	596	778	50	60	78	5	6	8	
6 000	7 154	9 337	600	715	934	60	72	93	6	7	9	
			700	835	1 089	70	83	109	7	8	11	Rise per 1000 Run = 649
			800	954	1 245	80	95	124	8	10	12	Ratio = 1:1.54
			900	1 073	1 401	90	107	140	9	11	14	

Hip Plumb Cut
Purlin Face Cut
Rafter Plumb Cut
Purlin Edge Cut
Hip Edge Cut
Jack R. Edge Cut
Rafter Seat Cut
Hip Seat Cut

Hip Seat Cut

Rafter Seat Cut

Jack R. Edge Cut

Hip Edge Cut

Purlin Edge Cut

Rafter Plumb Cut

Purlin Face Cut

Hip Plumb Cut

PITCH 34°	Run (mm)	Rafter Length	Hip Length	Run (mm)	Rafter Length	Hip Length	Run (mm)	Rafter Length	Hip Length	Run (mm)	Rafter Length	Hip Length
	1 000	1 206	1 567	100	121	157	10	12	16	1	1	2
	2 000	2 412	3 134	200	241	313	20	24	31	2	2	3
	3 000	3 619	4 700	300	362	470	30	36	47	3	4	5
	4 000	4 825	6 267	400	482	627	40	48	63	4	5	6
	5 000	6 031	7 834	500	603	783	50	60	78	5	6	8
	6 000	7 237	9 401	600	724	940	60	72	94	6	7	9
Rise per 1000 Run = 675				700	844	1 097	70	84	110	7	8	11
				800	965	1 253	80	96	125	8	10	13
Ratio = 1:1.48				900	1 086	1 410	90	109	141	9	11	14

PITCH 35°	Run (mm)	Rafter Length	Hip Length	Run (mm)	Rafter Length	Hip Length	Run (mm)	Rafter Length	Hip Length	Run (mm)	Rafter Length	Hip Length
	1 000	1 221	1 578	100	122	158	10	12	16	1	1	2
	2 000	2 442	3 156	200	244	316	20	24	32	2	2	3
	3 000	3 662	4 734	300	366	473	30	37	47	3	4	5
	4 000	4 883	6 312	400	488	631	40	49	63	4	5	6
	5 000	6 104	7 890	500	610	789	50	61	79	5	6	8
	6 000	7 325	9 468	600	732	947	60	73	95	6	7	9
Rise per 1000 Run = 700				700	855	1 105	70	85	110	7	9	11
				800	977	1 262	80	98	126	8	10	13
Ratio = 1:1.43				900	1 099	1 420	90	110	142	9	11	14

Hip Plumb Cut

Purlin Face Cut

Rafter Plumb Cut

Purlin Edge Cut

Hip Edge Cut

Jack R. Edge Cut

Rafter Seat Cut

Hip Seat Cut

Hip Seat Cut

Rafter Seat Cut

Jack R. Edge Cut

Hip Edge Cut

Purlin Edge Cut

Rafter Plumb Cut

Purlin Face Cut

Hip Plumb Cut

Run (mm)	Rafter Length	Hip Length	Run (mm)	Rafter Length	Hip Length	Run (mm)	Rafter Length	Hip Length	Run (mm)	Rafter Length	Hip Length	PITCH
1 000	1 236	1 590	100	124	159	10	12	16	1	1	2	**36°**
2 000	2 472	3 180	200	247	318	20	25	32	2	2	3	
3 000	3 708	4 770	300	371	477	30	37	48	3	4	5	
4 000	4 944	6 360	400	494	636	40	49	64	4	5	6	
5 000	6 180	7 950	500	618	795	50	62	79	5	6	8	
6 000	7 416	9 540	600	742	954	60	74	95	6	7	10	
			700	865	1 113	70	87	111	7	9	11	Rise per 1000 Run = 727
			800	989	1 272	80	99	127	8	10	13	Ratio = 1:1.38
			900	1 112	1 431	90	111	143	9	11	14	

Run (mm)	Rafter Length	Hip Length	Run (mm)	Rafter Length	Hip Length	Run (mm)	Rafter Length	Hip Length	Run (mm)	Rafter Length	Hip Length	PITCH
1 000	1 252	1 602	100	125	160	10	13	16	1	1	2	**37°**
2 000	2 504	3 205	200	250	320	20	25	32	2	2	3	
3 000	3 756	4 807	300	376	481	30	38	48	3	4	5	
4 000	5 009	6 410	400	501	641	40	50	64	4	5	6	
5 000	6 261	8 012	500	626	801	50	63	80	5	6	8	
6 000	7 513	9 615	600	751	961	60	75	96	6	8	10	
			700	876	1 122	70	88	112	7	9	11	Rise per 1000 Run = 754
			800	1 002	1 282	80	100	128	8	10	13	Ratio = 1:1.33
			900	1 127	1 442	90	113	144	9	11	14	

Hip Plumb Cut

Purlin Face Cut

Rafter Plumb Cut

Purlin Edge Cut

Hip Edge Cut

Jack R. Edge Cut

Rafter Seat Cut

Hip Seat Cut

Hip Seat Cut

Rafter Seat Cut

Jack R. Edge Cut

Hip Edge Cut

Purlin Edge Cut

Rafter Plumb Cut

Purlin Face Cut

Hip Plumb Cut

PITCH **38°**	Run (mm)	Rafter Length	Hip Length	Run (mm)	Rafter Length	Hip Length	Run (mm)	Rafter Length	Hip Length	Run (mm)	Rafter Length	Hip Length
	1 000	1 269	1 616	100	127	162	10	13	16	1	1	2
	2 000	2 538	3 231	200	254	323	20	25	32	2	3	3
	3 000	3 807	4 847	300	381	485	30	38	48	3	4	5
	4 000	5 076	6 463	400	508	646	40	51	65	4	5	6
	5 000	6 345	8 078	500	635	808	50	63	81	5	6	8
	6 000	7 614	9 694	600	761	969	60	76	97	6	8	10
Rise per 1000 Run = 781				700	888	1 131	70	89	113	7	9	11
				800	1 015	1 293	80	102	129	8	10	13
Ratio = 1:1.28				900	1 142	1 454	90	114	145	9	11	15

PITCH **39°**	Run (mm)	Rafter Length	Hip Length	Run (mm)	Rafter Length	Hip Length	Run (mm)	Rafter Length	Hip Length	Run (mm)	Rafter Length	Hip Length
	1 000	1 287	1 630	100	129	163	10	13	16	1	1	2
	2 000	2 574	3 259	200	257	326	20	26	33	2	3	3
	3 000	3 860	4 889	300	386	489	30	39	49	3	4	5
	4 000	5 147	6 519	400	515	652	40	51	65	4	5	7
	5 000	6 434	8 148	500	643	815	50	64	81	5	6	8
	6 000	7 721	9 778	600	772	978	60	77	98	6	8	10
Rise per 1000 Run = 810				700	901	1 141	70	90	114	7	9	11
				800	1 029	1 304	80	103	130	8	10	13
Ratio = 1:1.23				900	1 158	1 467	90	116	147	9	12	15

Hip Plumb Cut

Purlin Face Cut

Purlin Edge Cut

Rafter Plumb Cut

Hip Edge Cut

Rafter Seat Cut

Jack R. Edge Cut

Hip Seat Cut

Hip Seat Cut

Jack R. Edge Cut

Rafter Seat Cut

Hip Edge Cut

Rafter Plumb Cut

Purlin Edge Cut

Purlin Face Cut

Hip Plumb Cut

Run (mm)	Rafter Length	Hip Length	Run (mm)	Rafter Length	Hip Length	Run (mm)	Rafter Length	Hip Length	Run (mm)	Rafter Length	Hip Length	PITCH
1 000	1 305	1 644	100	131	164	10	13	16	1	1	2	**40°**
2 000	2 611	3 289	200	261	329	20	26	33	2	3	3	
3 000	3 916	4 933	300	392	493	30	39	49	3	4	5	
4 000	5 222	6 578	400	522	658	40	52	66	4	5	7	
5 000	6 527	8 222	500	653	822	50	65	82	5	7	8	
6 000	7 832	9 866	600	783	987	60	78	99	6	8	10	
			700	914	1 151	70	91	115	7	9	12	Rise per 1000 Run
			800	1 044	1 316	80	104	132	8	10	13	= 839
			900	1 175	1 480	90	117	148	9	12	15	Ratio = 1:1.19

Run (mm)	Rafter Length	Hip Length	Run (mm)	Rafter Length	Hip Length	Run (mm)	Rafter Length	Hip Length	Run (mm)	Rafter Length	Hip Length	PITCH
1 000	1 325	1 660	100	133	166	10	13	17	1	1	2	**41°**
2 000	2 650	3 320	200	265	332	20	27	33	2	3	3	
3 000	3 975	4 980	300	398	498	30	40	50	3	4	5	
4 000	5 300	6 640	400	530	664	40	53	66	4	5	7	
5 000	6 625	8 300	500	663	830	50	66	83	5	7	8	
6 000	7 950	9 960	600	795	996	60	80	100	6	8	10	
			700	928	1 162	70	93	116	7	9	12	Rise per 1000 Run
			800	1 060	1 328	80	106	133	8	11	13	= 869
			900	1 193	1 494	90	119	149	9	12	15	Ratio = 1:1.15

Hip Plumb Cut

Purlin Face Cut

Purlin Edge Cut

Rafter Plumb Cut

Rafter Seat Cut

Hip Edge Cut

Jack R. Edge Cut

Hip Seat Cut

Hip Seat Cut

Jack R. Edge Cut

Hip Edge Cut

Rafter Seat Cut

Rafter Plumb Cut

Purlin Edge Cut

Purlin Face Cut

Hip Plumb Cut

PITCH 42°

Rise per 1000 Run = 900
Ratio = 1:1.11

Run (mm)	Rafter Length	Hip Length	Run (mm)	Rafter Length	Hip Length	Run (mm)	Rafter Length	Hip Length	Run (mm)	Rafter Length	Hip Length
1 000	1 346	1 677	100	135	168	10	13	17	1	1	2
2 000	2 691	3 353	200	269	335	20	27	34	2	3	3
3 000	4 037	5 030	300	404	503	30	40	50	3	4	5
4 000	5 383	6 706	400	538	671	40	54	67	4	5	7
5 000	6 728	8 383	500	673	838	50	67	84	5	7	8
6 000	8 074	10 059	600	807	1 006	60	81	101	6	8	10
			700	942	1 174	70	94	117	7	9	12
			800	1 077	1 341	80	108	134	8	11	13
			900	1 211	1 509	90	121	151	9	12	15

PITCH 43°

Rise per 1000 Run = 933
Ratio = 1:1.07

Run (mm)	Rafter Length	Hip Length	Run (mm)	Rafter Length	Hip Length	Run (mm)	Rafter Length	Hip Length	Run (mm)	Rafter Length	Hip Length
1 000	1 367	1 694	100	137	169	10	14	17	1	1	2
2 000	2 735	3 388	200	273	339	20	27	34	2	3	3
3 000	4 102	5 082	300	410	508	30	41	51	3	4	5
4 000	5 469	6 776	400	547	678	40	55	68	4	5	7
5 000	6 837	8 470	500	684	847	50	68	85	5	7	8
6 000	8 204	10 164	600	820	1 016	60	82	102	6	8	10
			700	957	1 186	70	96	119	7	10	12
			800	1 094	1 355	80	109	136	8	11	14
			900	1 231	1 525	90	123	152	9	12	15

Hip Plumb Cut

Purlin Face Cut

Purlin Edge Cut

Rafter Plumb Cut

Rafter Seat Cut

Hip Edge Cut

Jack R. Edge Cut

Hip Seat Cut

Hip Seat Cut

Jack R. Edge Cut

Hip Edge Cut

Rafter Seat Cut

Rafter Plumb Cut

Purlin Edge Cut

Purlin Face Cut

Hip Plumb Cut

Run (mm)	Rafter Length	Hip Length	Run (mm)	Rafter Length	Hip Length	Run (mm)	Rafter Length	Hip Length	Run (mm)	Rafter Length	Hip Length	PITCH
1 000	1 390	1 712	100	139	171	10	14	17	1	1	2	**44°**
2 000	2 780	3 425	200	278	342	20	28	34	2	3	3	
3 000	4 170	5 137	300	417	514	30	42	51	3	4	5	
4 000	5 561	6 850	400	556	685	40	56	68	4	6	7	
5 000	6 951	8 562	500	695	856	50	70	86	5	7	9	
6 000	8 341	10 275	600	834	1 027	60	83	103	6	8	10	Rise per 1000 Run
			700	973	1 199	70	97	120	7	10	12	= 966
			800	1 112	1 370	80	111	137	8	11	14	Ratio = 1:1.04
			900	1 251	1 541	90	125	154	9	13	15	

Run (mm)	Rafter Length	Hip Length	Run (mm)	Rafter Length	Hip Length	Run (mm)	Rafter Length	Hip Length	Run (mm)	Rafter Length	Hip Length	PITCH
1 000	1 414	1 732	100	141	173	10	14	17	1	1	2	**45°**
2 000	2 828	3 464	200	283	346	20	28	35	2	3	3	
3 000	4 243	5 196	300	424	520	30	42	52	3	4	5	
4 000	5 657	6 928	400	566	693	40	57	69	4	6	7	
5 000	7 071	8 660	500	707	866	50	71	87	5	7	9	
6 000	8 485	10 392	600	849	1 039	60	85	104	6	8	10	Rise per 1000 Run
			700	990	1 212	70	99	121	7	10	12	= 1 000
			800	1 131	1 386	80	113	139	8	11	14	Ratio = 1:1.
			900	1 273	1 559	90	127	156	9	13	16	

Hip Plumb Cut

Purlin Face Cut

Purlin Edge Cut

Rafter Plumb Cut

Rafter Seat Cut

Hip Edge Cut

Jack R. Edge Cut

Hip Seat Cut

Jack R. Edge Cut
Hip Seat Cut
Hip Edge Cut
Rafter Plumb Cut
Rafter Seat Cut
Hip Plumb Cut
Purlin Face Cut
Purlin Edge Cut

PITCH 46°

Rise per 1000 Run = 1 036
Ratio = 1.04:1

Run (mm)	Rafter Length	Hip Length	Run (mm)	Rafter Length	Hip Length	Run (mm)	Rafter Length	Hip Length	Run (mm)	Rafter Length	Hip Length
1 000	1 440	1 753	100	144	175	10	14	18	1	1	2
2 000	2 879	3 506	200	288	351	20	29	35	2	3	4
3 000	4 319	5 258	300	432	526	30	43	53	3	4	5
4 000	5 758	7 011	400	576	701	40	58	70	4	6	7
5 000	7 198	8 764	500	720	876	50	72	88	5	7	9
6 000	8 637	10 517	600	864	1 052	60	86	105	6	9	11
			700	1 008	1 227	70	101	123	7	10	12
			800	1 152	1 402	80	115	140	8	12	14
			900	1 296	1 578	90	130	158	9	13	16

PITCH 47°

Rise per 1000 Run = 1 072
Ratio = 1.07:1

Run (mm)	Rafter Length	Hip Length	Run (mm)	Rafter Length	Hip Length	Run (mm)	Rafter Length	Hip Length	Run (mm)	Rafter Length	Hip Length
1 000	1 466	1 775	100	147	177	10	15	18	1	1	2
2 000	2 933	3 550	200	293	355	20	29	35	2	3	4
3 000	4 399	5 324	300	440	532	30	44	53	3	4	5
4 000	5 865	7 099	400	587	710	40	59	71	4	6	7
5 000	7 331	8 874	500	733	887	50	73	89	5	7	9
6 000	8 798	10 649	600	880	1 065	60	88	106	6	9	11
			700	1 026	1 242	70	103	124	7	10	12
			800	1 173	1 420	80	117	142	8	12	14
			900	1 320	1 597	90	132	160	9	13	16

Purlin Edge Cut
Purlin Face Cut
Hip Plumb Cut
Rafter Seat Cut
Rafter Plumb Cut
Hip Edge Cut
Hip Seat Cut
Jack R. Edge Cut

Run (mm)	Rafter Length	Hip Length	Run (mm)	Rafter Length	Hip Length	Run (mm)	Rafter Length	Hip Length	Run (mm)	Rafter Length	Hip Length	PITCH
1 000	1 494	1 798	100	149	180	10	15	18	1	1	2	
2 000	2 989	3 596	200	299	360	20	30	36	2	3	4	
3 000	4 483	5 395	300	448	539	30	45	54	3	4	5	**48°**
4 000	5 978	7 193	400	598	719	40	60	72	4	6	7	
5 000	7 472	8 991	500	747	899	50	75	90	5	7	9	
6 000	8 967	10 789	600	897	1 079	60	90	108	6	9	11	
			700	1 046	1 259	70	105	126	7	10	13	Rise per 1000 Run = 1 111
			800	1 196	1 439	80	120	144	8	12	14	Ratio = 1.11:1
			900	1 345	1 618	90	135	162	9	13	16	

Run (mm)	Rafter Length	Hip Length	Run (mm)	Rafter Length	Hip Length	Run (mm)	Rafter Length	Hip Length	Run (mm)	Rafter Length	Hip Length	PITCH
1 000	1 524	1 823	100	152	182	10	15	18	1	2	2	
2 000	3 049	3 646	200	305	365	20	30	36	2	3	4	
3 000	4 573	5 469	300	457	547	30	46	55	3	5	5	**49°**
4 000	6 097	7 292	400	610	729	40	61	73	4	6	7	
5 000	7 621	9 115	500	762	912	50	76	91	5	8	9	
6 000	9 146	10 938	600	915	1 094	60	91	109	6	9	11	
			700	1 067	1 276	70	107	128	7	11	13	Rise per 1000 Run = 1 150
			800	1 219	1 458	80	122	146	8	12	15	Ratio = 1.15:1
			900	1 372	1 641	90	137	164	9	14	16	

Jack R. Edge Cut

Hip Edge Cut

Hip Seat Cut

Rafter Plumb Cut

Rafter Seat Cut

Hip Plumb Cut

Purlin Face Cut

Purlin Edge Cut

PITCH 50°

Rise per 1000 Run = 1 192
Ratio = 1.19:1

Run (mm)	Rafter Length	Hip Length	Run (mm)	Rafter Length	Hip Length	Run (mm)	Rafter Length	Hip Length	Run (mm)	Rafter Length	Hip Length
1 000	1 556	1 849	100	156	185	10	16	18	1	2	2
2 000	3 111	3 699	200	311	370	20	31	37	2	3	4
3 000	4 667	5 548	300	467	555	30	47	55	3	5	6
4 000	6 223	7 398	400	622	740	40	62	74	4	6	7
5 000	7 779	9 247	500	778	925	50	78	92	5	8	9
6 000	9 334	11 096	600	933	1 110	60	93	111	6	9	11
			700	1 089	1 295	70	109	129	7	11	13
			800	1 245	1 480	80	124	148	8	12	15
			900	1 400	1 664	90	140	166	9	14	17

PITCH 51°

Rise per 1000 Run = 1 235
Ratio = 1.23:1

Run (mm)	Rafter Length	Hip Length	Run (mm)	Rafter Length	Hip Length	Run (mm)	Rafter Length	Hip Length	Run (mm)	Rafter Length	Hip Length
1 000	1 589	1 877	100	159	188	10	16	19	1	2	2
2 000	3 178	3 755	200	318	375	20	32	38	2	3	4
3 000	4 767	5 632	300	477	563	30	48	56	3	5	6
4 000	6 356	7 510	400	636	751	40	64	75	4	6	8
5 000	7 945	9 387	500	795	939	50	79	94	5	8	9
6 000	9 534	11 265	600	953	1 126	60	95	113	6	10	11
			700	1 112	1 314	70	111	131	7	11	13
			800	1 271	1 502	80	127	150	8	13	15
			900	1 430	1 690	90	143	169	9	14	17

Purlin Edge Cut

Purlin Face Cut

Rafter Seat Cut

Hip Plumb Cut

Hip Seat Cut

Rafter Plumb Cut

Hip Edge Cut

Jack R. Edge Cut

Jack R. Edge Cut
Hip Edge Cut
Rafter Plumb Cut
Hip Seat Cut
Hip Plumb Cut
Rafter Seat Cut
Purlin Face Cut
Purlin Edge Cut

Run (mm)	Rafter Length	Hip Length	Run (mm)	Rafter Length	Hip Length	Run (mm)	Rafter Length	Hip Length	Run (mm)	Rafter Length	Hip Length	PITCH
1 000	1 624	1 907	100	162	191	10	16	19	1	2	2	**52°**
2 000	3 249	3 815	200	325	381	20	32	38	2	3	4	
3 000	4 873	5 722	300	487	572	30	49	57	3	5	6	
4 000	6 497	7 630	400	650	763	40	65	76	4	6	8	
5 000	8 121	9 537	500	812	954	50	81	95	5	8	10	
6 000	9 746	11 445	600	975	1 144	60	97	114	6	10	11	
			700	1 137	1 335	70	114	134	7	11	13	Rise per 1000 Run
			800	1 299	1 526	80	130	153	8	13	15	= 1 280
			900	1 462	1 717	90	146	172	9	15	17	Ratio = 1.28:1

Run (mm)	Rafter Length	Hip Length	Run (mm)	Rafter Length	Hip Length	Run (mm)	Rafter Length	Hip Length	Run (mm)	Rafter Length	Hip Length	PITCH
1 000	1 662	1 939	100	166	194	10	17	19	1	2	2	**53°**
2 000	3 323	3 879	200	332	388	20	33	39	2	3	4	
3 000	4 985	5 818	300	498	582	30	50	58	3	5	6	
4 000	6 647	7 757	400	665	776	40	66	78	4	7	8	
5 000	8 308	9 697	500	831	970	50	83	97	5	8	10	
6 000	9 970	11 636	600	997	1 164	60	100	116	6	10	12	
			700	1 163	1 358	70	116	136	7	12	14	Rise per 1000 Run
			800	1 329	1 551	80	133	155	8	13	16	= 1 327
			900	1 495	1 745	90	150	175	9	15	17	Ratio = 1.33:1

Purlin Edge Cut
Rafter Seat Cut
Purlin Face Cut
Hip Plumb Cut
Hip Seat Cut
Rafter Plumb Cut
Hip Edge Cut
Jack R. Edge Cut

Jack R. Edge Cut

Hip Edge Cut

Rafter Plumb Cut

Hip Seat Cut

Hip Plumb Cut

Purlin Face Cut

Rafter Seat Cut

Purlin Edge Cut

PITCH **54°** Rise per 1000 Run = 1 376 Ratio = 1.38:1	Run (mm)	Rafter Length	Hip Length	Run (mm)	Rafter Length	Hip Length	Run (mm)	Rafter Length	Hip Length	Run (mm)	Rafter Length	Hip Length
	1 000	1 701	1 973	100	170	197	10	17	20	1	2	2
	2 000	3 403	3 947	200	340	395	20	34	39	2	3	4
	3 000	5 104	5 920	300	510	592	30	51	59	3	5	6
	4 000	6 805	7 894	400	681	789	40	68	79	4	7	8
	5 000	8 507	9 867	500	851	987	50	85	99	5	9	10
	6 000	10 208	11 841	600	1 021	1 184	60	102	118	6	10	12
				700	1 191	1 381	70	119	138	7	12	14
				800	1 361	1 579	80	136	158	8	14	16
				900	1 531	1 776	90	153	178	9	15	18

PITCH **55°** Rise per 1000 Run = 1 428 Ratio = 1.43:1	Run (mm)	Rafter Length	Hip Length	Run (mm)	Rafter Length	Hip Length	Run (mm)	Rafter Length	Hip Length	Run (mm)	Rafter Length	Hip Length
	1 000	1 743	2 010	100	174	201	10	17	20	1	2	2
	2 000	3 487	4 020	200	349	402	20	35	40	2	3	4
	3 000	5 230	6 030	300	523	603	30	52	60	3	5	6
	4 000	6 974	8 040	400	697	804	40	70	80	4	7	8
	5 000	8 717	10 049	500	872	1 005	50	87	100	5	9	10
	6 000	10 461	12 059	600	1 046	1 206	60	105	121	6	10	12
				700	1 220	1 407	70	122	141	7	12	14
				800	1 395	1 608	80	139	161	8	14	16
				900	1 569	1 809	90	157	181	9	16	18

Purlin Edge Cut

Rafter Seat Cut

Purlin Face Cut

Hip Seat Cut

Hip Plumb Cut

Hip Edge Cut

Rafter Plumb Cut

Jack R. Edge Cut

Jack R. Edge Cut

Rafter Plumb Cut

Hip Edge Cut

Hip Plumb Cut

Hip Seat Cut

Purlin Face Cut

Rafter Seat Cut

Purlin Edge Cut

Run (mm)	Rafter Length	Hip Length	Run (mm)	Rafter Length	Hip Length	Run (mm)	Rafter Length	Hip Length	Run (mm)	Rafter Length	Hip Length	PITCH
1 000	1 788	2 049	100	179	205	10	18	20	1	2	2	**56°**
2 000	3 577	4 098	200	358	410	20	36	41	2	4	4	
3 000	5 365	6 147	300	536	615	30	54	61	3	5	6	
4 000	7 153	8 196	400	715	820	40	72	82	4	7	8	
5 000	8 941	10 244	500	894	1 024	50	89	102	5	9	10	
6 000	10 730	12 293	600	1 073	1 229	60	107	123	6	11	12	Rise per 1000 Run
			700	1 252	1 434	70	125	143	7	13	14	= 1 483
			800	1 431	1 639	80	143	164	8	14	16	Ratio = 1.48:1
			900	1 609	1 844	90	161	184	9	16	18	

Run (mm)	Rafter Length	Hip Length	Run (mm)	Rafter Length	Hip Length	Run (mm)	Rafter Length	Hip Length	Run (mm)	Rafter Length	Hip Length	PITCH
1 000	1 836	2 091	100	184	209	10	18	21	1	2	2	**57°**
2 000	3 672	4 181	200	367	418	20	37	42	2	4	4	
3 000	5 508	6 272	300	551	627	30	55	63	3	6	6	
4 000	7 344	8 363	400	734	836	40	73	84	4	7	8	
5 000	9 180	10 454	500	918	1 045	50	92	105	5	9	10	
6 000	11 016	12 544	600	1 102	1 254	60	110	125	6	11	13	Rise per 1000 Run
			700	1 285	1 464	70	129	146	7	13	15	= 1 540
			800	1 469	1 672	80	147	167	8	15	17	Ratio = 1.54:1
			900	1 652	1 882	90	165	188	9	17	19	

Purlin Edge Cut

Rafter Seat Cut

Purlin Face Cut

Hip Seat Cut

Hip Plumb Cut

Hip Edge Cut

Rafter Plumb Cut

Jack R. Edge Cut

Jack R. Edge Cut
Rafter Plumb Cut
Hip Edge Cut
Hip Plumb Cut
Hip Seat Cut
Purlin Face Cut
Rafter Seat Cut
Purlin Edge Cut

PITCH 58°	Run (mm)	Rafter Length	Hip Length	Run (mm)	Rafter Length	Hip Length	Run (mm)	Rafter Length	Hip Length	Run (mm)	Rafter Length	Hip Length
Rise per 1000 Run = 1 600 Ratio = 1.6:1	1 000	1 887	2 136	100	189	214	10	19	21	1	2	2
	2 000	3 774	4 271	200	377	427	20	38	43	2	4	4
	3 000	5 661	6 407	300	566	641	30	57	64	3	6	6
	4 000	7 548	8 543	400	755	854	40	75	85	4	8	9
	5 000	9 435	10 678	500	944	1 068	50	94	107	5	9	11
	6 000	11 322	12 814	600	1 132	1 281	60	113	128	6	11	13
				700	1 321	1 495	70	132	149	7	13	15
				800	1 510	1 709	80	151	171	8	15	17
				900	1 698	1 922	90	170	192	9	17	19

PITCH 59°	Run (mm)	Rafter Length	Hip Length	Run (mm)	Rafter Length	Hip Length	Run (mm)	Rafter Length	Hip Length	Run (mm)	Rafter Length	Hip Length
Rise per 1000 Run = 1 664 Ratio = 1.66:1	1 000	1 942	2 184	100	194	218	10	19	22	1	2	2
	2 000	3 883	4 368	200	388	437	20	39	44	2	4	4
	3 000	5 825	6 552	300	582	655	30	58	66	3	6	7
	4 000	7 766	8 736	400	777	874	40	78	87	4	8	9
	5 000	9 708	10 920	500	971	1 092	50	97	109	5	10	11
	6 000	11 650	13 104	600	1 165	1 310	60	116	131	6	12	13
				700	1 359	1 529	70	136	153	7	14	15
				800	1 553	1 747	80	155	175	8	16	17
				900	1 747	1 966	90	175	197	9	17	20

Purlin Edge Cut
Rafter Seat Cut
Purlin Face Cut
Hip Seat Cut
Hip Plumb Cut
Hip Edge Cut
Rafter Plumb Cut
Jack R. Edge Cut

Jack R. Edge Cut

Rafter Plumb Cut

Hip Edge Cut

Hip Plumb Cut

Purlin Face Cut

Hip Seat Cut

Rafter Seat Cut

Purlin Edge Cut

Run (mm)	Rafter Length	Hip Length	Run (mm)	Rafter Length	Hip Length	Run (mm)	Rafter Length	Hip Length	Run (mm)	Rafter Length	Hip Length
1 000	2 000	2 236	100	200	224	10	20	22	1	2	2
2 000	4 000	4 472	200	400	447	20	40	45	2	4	4
3 000	6 000	6 708	300	600	671	30	60	67	3	6	7
4 000	8 000	8 944	400	800	894	40	80	89	4	8	9
5 000	10 000	11 180	500	1 000	1 118	50	100	112	5	10	11
6 000	12 000	13 416	600	1 200	1 342	60	120	134	6	12	13
			700	1 400	1 565	70	140	157	7	14	16
			800	1 600	1 789	80	160	179	8	16	18
			900	1 800	2 012	90	180	201	9	18	20

PITCH

60°

Rise per 1000 Run
= 1 732
Ratio = 1.73:1

Run (mm)	Rafter Length	Hip Length	Run (mm)	Rafter Length	Hip Length	Run (mm)	Rafter Length	Hip Length	Run (mm)	Rafter Length	Hip Length
1 000	2 063	2 292	100	206	229	10	21	23	1	2	2
2 000	4 125	4 585	200	413	458	20	41	46	2	4	5
3 000	6 188	6 877	300	619	688	30	62	69	3	6	7
4 000	8 251	9 169	400	825	917	40	83	92	4	8	9
5 000	10 313	11 461	500	1 031	1 146	50	103	115	5	10	11
6 000	12 376	13 754	600	1 238	1 375	60	124	138	6	12	14
			700	1 444	1 605	70	144	160	7	14	16
			800	1 650	1 834	80	165	183	8	17	18
			900	1 856	2 063	90	186	206	9	19	21

PITCH

61°

Rise per 1000 Run
= 1 804
Ratio = 1.8:1

Purlin Edge Cut

Rafter Seat Cut

Hip Seat Cut

Purlin Face Cut

Hip Plumb Cut

Hip Edge Cut

Rafter Plumb Cut

Jack R. Edge Cut

Jack R. Edge Cut

Rafter Plumb Cut

Hip Edge Cut

Hip Plumb Cut

Purlin Face Cut

Hip Seat Cut

Rafter Seat Cut

Purlin Edge Cut

PITCH

62°

Rise per 1000 Run = 1 881
Ratio = 1.88:1

Run (mm)	Rafter Length	Hip Length	Run (mm)	Rafter Length	Hip Length	Run (mm)	Rafter Length	Hip Length	Run (mm)	Rafter Length	Hip Length
1 000	2 130	2 353	100	213	235	10	21	24	1	2	2
2 000	4 260	4 706	200	426	471	20	43	47	2	4	5
3 000	6 390	7 059	300	639	706	30	64	71	3	6	7
4 000	8 520	9 412	400	852	941	40	85	94	4	8	9
5 000	10 650	11 766	500	1 065	1 177	50	107	118	5	11	12
6 000	12 780	14 119	600	1 278	1 412	60	128	141	6	13	14
			700	1 491	1 647	70	149	165	7	15	16
			800	1 704	1 882	80	170	188	8	17	19
			900	1 917	2 118	90	192	212	9	19	21

PITCH

63°

Rise per 1000 Run = 1 963
Ratio = 1.96:1

Run (mm)	Rafter Length	Hip Length	Run (mm)	Rafter Length	Hip Length	Run (mm)	Rafter Length	Hip Length	Run (mm)	Rafter Length	Hip Length
1 000	2 203	2 419	100	220	242	10	22	24	1	2	2
2 000	4 405	4 838	200	441	484	20	44	48	2	4	5
3 000	6 608	7 257	300	661	726	30	66	73	3	7	7
4 000	8 811	9 676	400	881	968	40	88	97	4	9	10
5 000	11 013	12 095	500	1 101	1 210	50	110	121	5	11	12
6 000	13 216	14 514	600	1 322	1 451	60	132	145	6	13	15
			700	1 542	1 693	70	154	169	7	15	17
			800	1 762	1 935	80	176	194	8	18	19
			900	1 982	2 177	90	198	218	9	20	22

Purlin Edge Cut

Rafter Seat Cut

Hip Seat Cut

Purlin Face Cut

Hip Plumb Cut

Hip Edge Cut

Rafter Plumb Cut

Jack R. Edge Cut

Jack R. Edge Cut

Rafter Plumb Cut

Hip Edge Cut

Hip Plumb Cut

Purlin Face Cut

Hip Seat Cut

Rafter Seat Cut

Purlin Edge Cut

Run (mm)	Rafter Length	Hip Length	Run (mm)	Rafter Length	Hip Length	Run (mm)	Rafter Length	Hip Length	Run (mm)	Rafter Length	Hip Length	PITCH
1 000	2 281	2 491	100	228	249	10	23	25	1	2	2	**64°**
2 000	4 562	4 981	200	456	498	20	46	50	2	4	5	
3 000	6 844	7 472	300	684	747	30	68	75	3	7	7	
4 000	9 125	9 963	400	912	996	40	91	100	4	9	10	
5 000	11 406	12 454	500	1 141	1 245	50	114	125	5	11	12	
6 000	13 687	14 944	600	1 369	1 494	60	137	149	6	14	15	Rise per 1000 Run
			700	1 597	1 744	70	160	174	7	16	17	= 2 050
			800	1 825	1 993	80	182	199	8	18	20	Ratio = 2.05:1
			900	2 053	2 242	90	205	224	9	21	22	

Run (mm)	Rafter Length	Hip Length	Run (mm)	Rafter Length	Hip Length	Run (mm)	Rafter Length	Hip Length	Run (mm)	Rafter Length	Hip Length	PITCH
1 000	2 366	2 569	100	237	257	10	24	26	1	2	3	**65°**
2 000	4 732	5 138	200	473	514	20	47	51	2	5	5	
3 000	7 099	7 707	300	710	771	30	71	77	3	7	8	
4 000	9 465	10 275	400	946	1 028	40	95	103	4	9	10	
5 000	11 831	12 844	500	1 183	1 284	50	118	128	5	12	13	
6 000	14 197	15 413	600	1 420	1 541	60	142	154	6	14	15	Rise per 1000 Run
			700	1 656	1 798	70	166	180	7	17	18	= 2 145
			800	1 893	2 055	80	189	206	8	19	21	Ratio = 2.14:1
			900	2 130	2 312	90	213	231	9	21	23	

Purlin Edge Cut

Rafter Seat Cut

Hip Seat Cut

Purlin Face Cut

Hip Plumb Cut

Hip Edge Cut

Rafter Plumb Cut

Jack R. Edge Cut

Jack R. Edge Cut

Rafter Plumb Cut

Hip Edge Cut

Hip Plumb Cut

Purlin Face Cut

Hip Seat Cut

Rafter Seat Cut

Purlin Edge Cut

PITCH **66°**	Run (mm)	Rafter Length	Hip Length	Run (mm)	Rafter Length	Hip Length	Run (mm)	Rafter Length	Hip Length	Run (mm)	Rafter Length	Hip Length
	1 000	2 459	2 654	100	246	265	10	25	27	1	2	3
	2 000	4 917	5 308	200	492	531	20	49	53	2	5	5
	3 000	7 376	7 963	300	738	796	30	74	80	3	7	8
	4 000	9 834	10 617	400	983	1 062	40	98	106	4	10	11
	5 000	12 293	13 271	500	1 229	1 327	50	123	133	5	12	13
	6 000	14 752	15 925	600	1 475	1 593	60	148	159	6	15	16
Rise per 1000 Run = 2 246				700	1 721	1 858	70	172	186	7	17	19
Ratio = 2.25:1				800	1 967	2 123	80	197	212	8	20	21
				900	2 213	2 389	90	221	239	9	22	24

PITCH **67°**	Run (mm)	Rafter Length	Hip Length	Run (mm)	Rafter Length	Hip Length	Run (mm)	Rafter Length	Hip Length	Run (mm)	Rafter Length	Hip Length
	1 000	2 559	2 748	100	256	275	10	26	27	1	2	3
	2 000	5 119	5 495	200	512	550	20	51	55	2	5	5
	3 000	7 678	8 243	300	768	824	30	77	82	3	8	8
	4 000	10 237	10 991	400	1 024	1 099	40	102	110	4	10	11
	5 000	12 797	13 739	500	1 280	1 374	50	128	137	5	13	14
	6 000	15 356	16 486	600	1 536	1 649	60	154	165	6	15	16
Rise per 1000 Run = 2 356				700	1 792	1 923	70	179	192	7	18	19
Ratio = 2.36:1				800	2 047	2 198	80	205	220	8	20	22
				900	2 303	2 473	90	230	247	9	23	25

Purlin Edge Cut

Rafter Seat Cut

Hip Seat Cut

Purlin Face Cut

Hip Plumb Cut

Hip Edge Cut

Rafter Plumb Cut

Jack R. Edge Cut

Jack R. Edge Cut

Rafter Plumb Cut

Hip Edge Cut

Hip Plumb Cut

Purlin Face Cut

Hip Seat Cut

Rafter Seat Cut

Purlin Edge Cut

Run (mm)	Rafter Length	Hip Length	Run (mm)	Rafter Length	Hip Length	Run (mm)	Rafter Length	Hip Length	Run (mm)	Rafter Length	Hip Length	PITCH
1 000	2 669	2 851	100	267	285	10	27	29	1	3	3	**68°**
2 000	5 339	5 701	200	534	570	20	53	57	2	5	6	
3 000	8 008	8 552	300	801	855	30	80	86	3	8	9	
4 000	10 678	11 402	400	1 068	1 140	40	107	114	4	11	11	
5 000	13 347	14 253	500	1 335	1 425	50	133	143	5	13	14	
6 000	16 017	17 104	600	1 602	1 710	60	160	171	6	16	17	
			700	1 869	1 995	70	187	200	7	19	20	Rise per 1000 Run
			800	2 136	2 280	80	214	228	8	21	23	= 2 475
			900	2 403	2 566	90	240	257	9	24	26	Ratio = 2.48:1

Run (mm)	Rafter Length	Hip Length	Run (mm)	Rafter Length	Hip Length	Run (mm)	Rafter Length	Hip Length	Run (mm)	Rafter Length	Hip Length	PITCH
1 000	2 790	2 964	100	279	296	10	28	30	1	3	3	**69°**
2 000	5 581	5 928	200	558	593	20	56	59	2	6	6	
3 000	8 371	8 893	300	837	889	30	84	89	3	8	9	
4 000	11 162	11 857	400	1 116	1 186	40	112	119	4	11	12	
5 000	13 952	14 821	500	1 395	1 482	50	140	148	5	14	15	
6 000	16 743	17 785	600	1 674	1 779	60	167	178	6	17	18	
			700	1 953	2 075	70	195	207	7	20	21	Rise per 1000 Run
			800	2 232	2 371	80	223	237	8	22	24	= 2 605
			900	2 511	2 668	90	251	267	9	25	27	Ratio = 2.61:1

Purlin Edge Cut

Rafter Seat Cut

Hip Seat Cut

Purlin Face Cut

Hip Plumb Cut

Hip Edge Cut

Rafter Plumb Cut

Jack R. Edge Cut

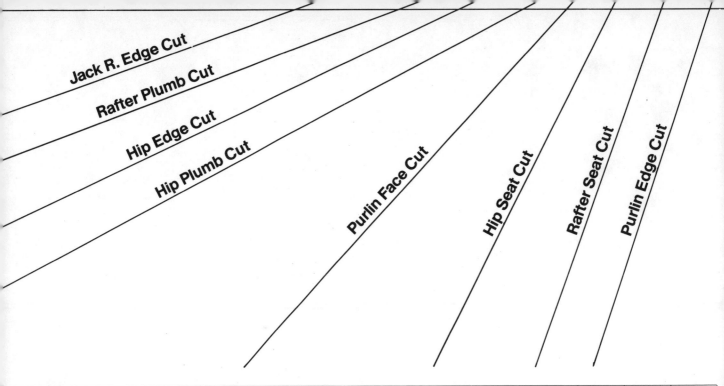

PITCH **70°**	Run (mm)	Rafter Length	Hip Length	Run (mm)	Rafter Length	Hip Length	Run (mm)	Rafter Length	Hip Length	Run (mm)	Rafter Length	Hip Length
	1 000	2 924	3 090	100	292	309	10	29	31	1	3	3
	2 000	5 848	6 180	200	585	618	20	58	62	2	6	6
	3 000	8 771	9 270	300	877	927	30	88	93	3	9	9
	4 000	11 695	12 360	400	1 170	1 236	40	117	124	4	12	12
	5 000	14 619	15 450	500	1 462	1 545	50	146	155	5	15	15
Rise per 1000 Run = 2 747 Ratio = 2.75:1	6 000	17 543	18 540	600	1 754	1 854	60	175	185	6	18	19
				700	2 047	2 163	70	205	216	7	20	22
				800	2 339	2 472	80	234	247	8	23	25
				900	2 631	2 781	90	263	278	9	26	28

PITCH **71°**	Run (mm)	Rafter Length	Hip Length	Run (mm)	Rafter Length	Hip Length	Run (mm)	Rafter Length	Hip Length	Run (mm)	Rafter Length	Hip Length
	1 000	3 072	3 230	100	307	323	10	31	32	1	3	3
	2 000	6 143	6 460	200	614	646	20	61	65	2	6	6
	3 000	9 215	9 691	300	921	969	30	92	97	3	9	10
	4 000	12 286	12 921	400	1 229	1 292	40	123	129	4	12	13
	5 000	15 358	16 151	500	1 536	1 615	50	154	162	5	15	16
Rise per 1000 Run = 2 904 Ratio = 2.9:1	6 000	18 429	19 381	600	1 843	1 938	60	184	194	6	18	19
				700	2 150	2 261	70	215	226	7	22	23
				800	2 457	2 584	80	246	258	8	25	26
				900	2 764	2 907	90	276	291	9	28	29

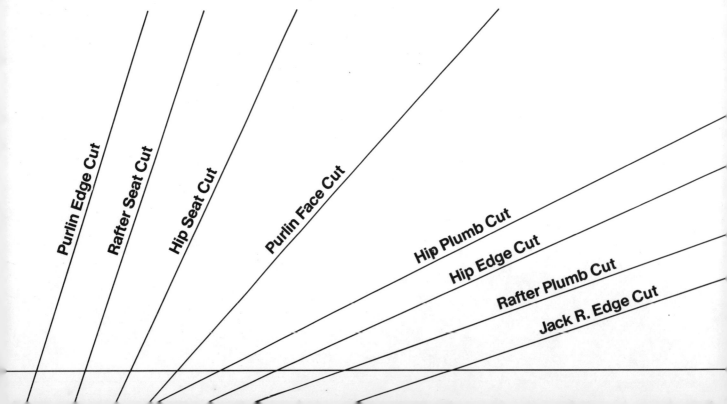

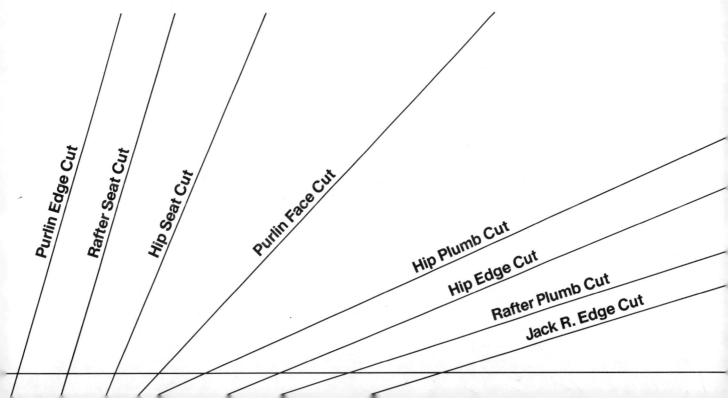

Jack R. Edge Cut

Rafter Plumb Cut

Hip Edge Cut

Hip Plumb Cut

Purlin Face Cut

Hip Seat Cut

Rafter Seat Cut

Purlin Edge Cut

Run (mm)	Rafter Length	Hip Length	Run (mm)	Rafter Length	Hip Length	Run (mm)	Rafter Length	Hip Length	Run (mm)	Rafter Length	Hip Length	PITCH
1 000	3 236	3 387	100	324	339	10	32	34	1	3	3	**72°**
2 000	6 472	6 774	200	647	677	20	65	68	2	6	7	
3 000	9 708	10 161	300	971	1 016	30	97	102	3	10	10	
4 000	12 944	13 548	400	1 294	1 355	40	129	135	4	13	14	
5 000	16 180	16 935	500	1 618	1 694	50	162	169	5	16	17	
6 000	19 416	20 322	600	1 942	2 032	60	194	203	6	19	20	Rise per 1000 Run = 3 078
			700	2 265	2 371	70	227	237	7	23	24	Ratio = 3.08:1
			800	2 589	2 710	80	259	271	8	26	27	
			900	2 912	3 048	90	291	305	9	29	30	

Run (mm)	Rafter Length	Hip Length	Run (mm)	Rafter Length	Hip Length	Run (mm)	Rafter Length	Hip Length	Run (mm)	Rafter Length	Hip Length	PITCH
1 000	3 420	3 563	100	342	356	10	34	36	1	3	4	**73°**
2 000	6 841	7 127	200	684	713	20	68	71	2	7	7	
3 000	10 261	10 690	300	1 026	1 069	30	103	107	3	10	11	
4 000	13 681	14 254	400	1 368	1 425	40	137	143	4	14	14	
5 000	17 102	17 817	500	1 710	1 782	50	171	178	5	17	18	
6 000	20 522	21 381	600	2 052	2 138	60	205	214	6	21	21	Rise per 1000 Run = 3 271
			700	2 394	2 494	70	239	249	7	24	25	Ratio = 3.27:1
			800	2 736	2 851	80	274	285	8	27	29	
			900	3 078	3 207	90	308	321	9	31	32	

Purlin Edge Cut

Rafter Seat Cut

Hip Seat Cut

Purlin Face Cut

Hip Plumb Cut

Hip Edge Cut

Rafter Plumb Cut

Jack R. Edge Cut

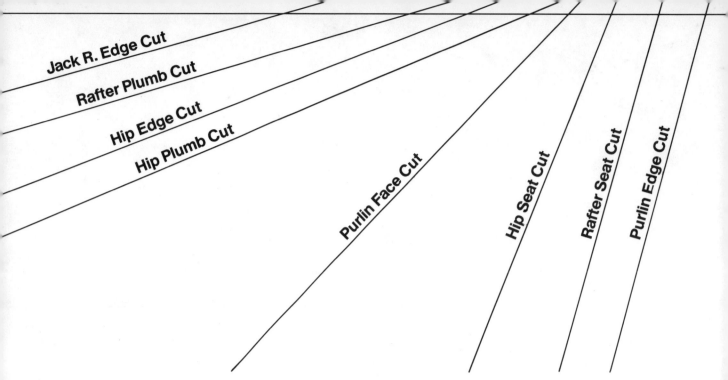

PITCH 74°	Run (mm)	Rafter Length	Hip Length	Run (mm)	Rafter Length	Hip Length	Run (mm)	Rafter Length	Hip Length	Run (mm)	Rafter Length	Hip Length
	1 000	3 628	3 763	100	363	376	10	36	38	1	4	4
	2 000	7 256	7 526	200	726	753	20	73	75	2	7	8
	3 000	10 884	11 290	300	1 088	1 129	30	109	113	3	11	11
	4 000	14 512	15 053	400	1 451	1 505	40	145	151	4	15	15
	5 000	18 140	18 816	500	1 814	1 882	50	181	188	5	18	19
	6 000	21 768	22 579	600	2 177	2 258	60	218	226	6	22	23
Rise per 1000 Run = 3 487 Ratio = 3.49:1				700	2 540	2 634	70	254	263	7	25	26
				800	2 902	3 011	80	290	301	8	29	30
				900	3 265	3 387	90	327	339	9	33	34

PITCH 75°	Run (mm)	Rafter Length	Hip Length	Run (mm)	Rafter Length	Hip Length	Run (mm)	Rafter Length	Hip Length	Run (mm)	Rafter Length	Hip Length
	1 000	3 864	3 991	100	386	399	10	39	40	1	4	4
	2 000	7 727	7 982	200	773	798	20	77	80	2	8	8
	3 000	11 591	11 973	300	1 159	1 197	30	116	120	3	12	12
	4 000	15 455	15 964	400	1 545	1 596	40	155	160	4	15	16
	5 000	19 319	19 955	500	1 932	1 996	50	193	200	5	19	20
	6 000	23 182	23 946	600	2 318	2 395	60	232	239	6	23	24
Rise per 1000 Run = 3 732 Ratio = 3.73:1				700	2 705	2 794	70	270	279	7	27	28
				800	3 091	3 193	80	309	319	8	31	32
				900	3 477	3 592	90	348	359	9	35	36

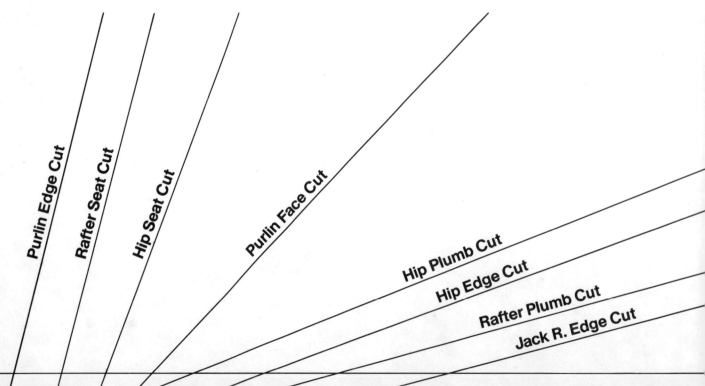

Clearly illustrated and easy to understand: gives large birdseye views of each building procedure: practical advice on how to identify and correct faulty building practice. Shows the correct trade terms for ordering timber, concrete etc. Detailed section on adding on a room: buying a house to renovate: restumping, even raising up a house.

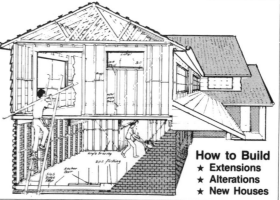

How to be
A Successful
Owner Builder
& Renovator

How to Build
★ Extensions
★ Alterations
★ New Houses

The Companion
to The Australian
Owner Builders Manual

Allan Staines

The Australian
Owner Builders
Manual

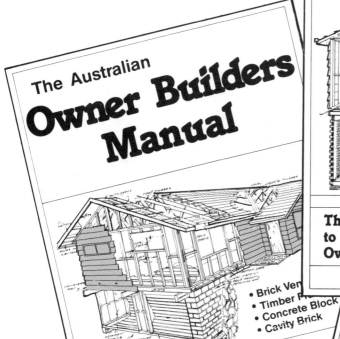

• Brick Ven...
• Timber F...
• Concrete Block
• Cavity Brick

Over 400
illustrations

Step by Step Guide to Building
Your Own Home.

Allan Staines

An essential guide on the building site: describes framing procedures in detail and gives trade hints and tips. A most easy to follow manual.

The Australian
Roof Building
Manual

With
Tables
& Bevels

The Easy Step by Step Guide
to Building a Roof

Lloyd Hiddle & Allan Staines

This step by step guide is full of easy to follow instructions: an indispensible aid for teaching apprentices: plus the new quick and easy to use tables & bevels for all roof pitches from 5 degrees to 75 degrees. Bevels drawn on the page ready to transfer directly to the bevel tool: a builder's dream.

Pinedale  Books

2 Lethbridge Ct, Caloundra Qld 4551 Aust.

The Australian
Renovator's Manual

- Attics
- Kitchens
- Tiling
- Windows
- Doors
- Lots More

A must for tradesmen & home owners

The material in this book is not included in any of the other manuals in the Owner Builder Series.

The Easy Step by Step Guide to Home Renovations

Allan Staines

This book is specifically designed to deal with problems confronted when renovating or altering an existing dwelling. It also shows step-by-step how to accomplish popular renovation projects. It solves problems such as how to support the roof when making openings in walls how to support a proposed attic; installing skylights; guttering; shelving; replacing existing floor joists; flooring; fixing sagging roof rafters; installing french doors or windows into most types of walls; building carports; decks; flyscreens; cat doors; stormwater drains; how to laminate; fitting panelling to shower recesses.

Pinedale Books

2 Lethbridge Court, Caloundra, 4551 Qld. Australia.